EDUCATION MATTERS

General Editor: Ted Wragg

SECONDARY EDUCATION

GW00702003

BOOKS IN THIS SERIES

SECONDARY EDUCATION

Maureen O'Connor

CASSELL

Cassell Educational Ltd
Villiers House,
41/47 Strand
London WC2N 5JE, England

© Cassell Educational Limited 1990

First published 1990

British Library Cataloguing in Publication Data
O'Connor, Maureen, *1940–*
  Secondary education. — (Education matters).
  1. Great Britain. Secondary education, history
  I. Title   II. Series
  373.41

ISBN 0–304–31951–1 (hardback)
       0–304–31956–2 (paperback)

Phototypeset by Input Typesetting Ltd, London

Printed and bound in Great Britain by
Biddles Ltd, Guildford and King's Lynn

CONTENTS

FOREWORD

During the 1980s a succession of Education Acts changed considerably the nature of schools and their relationships with the outside world. Parents were given more rights and responsibilities, including the opportunity to serve on the governing body of their child's school. The 1988 Education Act in particular, by introducing for the first time a National Curriculum, the testing of children at the ages of 7, 11, 14 and 16, local management, including financial responsibility and the creation of new types of school, was a radical break with the past. Furthermore the disappearance of millions of jobs, along with other changes in our society, led to reforms not only of schools, but also of further and higher education.

In the wake of such rapid and substantial changes it was not just parents and lay people, but also teachers and other professionals working in education, who found themselves struggling to keep up with what these many changes meant and how to get the best out of them. The *Education Matters* series addresses directly the major topics of reform, such as the new curriculum, testing and assessment, the role of parents and the handling of school finances, considering their effects on primary, secondary, further and higher education, and also the continuing education of adults.

The aim of the series is to present information about the challenges facing education in the remainder of the twentieth century in an authoritative but readable form. The books in the series, therefore, are of particular interest to parents, governors and all those concerned with education, but are written in such a way as to give an overview to students, experienced teachers and other professionals who work in the field.

Each book gives an account of the relevant legislation and background, but, more importantly, stresses practical implications of change with specific examples of what is being or can be done to make reforms work effectively. The authors are not only authorities in their field, but also have direct experience of the matters they write about. That is why the *Education Matters* series makes an important contribution to both debate and practice.

Professor E. C. Wragg,
Exeter University

For John Fairhall, the best of colleagues and friends

INTRODUCTION

In 1964 I found myself, an untrained graduate, temporarily in charge of a class of 11-year-old girls in a secondary modern school in the south-west of England. The fact that I could knock on the education authority's door and be standing, without any preparation as a teacher, in front of a class a few days later is a measure of the acute shortage of teachers which existed at that time, even in the most attractive parts of the country.

Even more significant, I thought then, and still believe, was the attitude of the girls, who greeted my arrival with great interest and the uninhibited friendliness of children who had just moved up from primary school. 'You don't need to bother about us, Miss', they assured me as I told them I had been asked by their headmistress to attempt to teach them a little basic English grammar. 'All the bright ones have gone up the road to the grammar school.'

At the age of 11 these little girls, bright-eyed and well turned-out, found themselves in a relatively modern, though pretty bleak, school building which boasted a single science lab, and that with a leaky roof. They had been assessed as failures by the 11-plus examination, and then still further streamed by their new school, and had written themselves off educationally for good.

That, I was convinced then and remain convinced after 25 years of writing about education and visiting, I suppose, some hundreds of schools all over the country, remains the English disease in secondary education. Not only had the system, with the combined wisdom of all its psychologists and administrators and teachers, written those children off, but they had very comprehensively been persuaded to write themselves off as well. Since the abolition of the 11-plus the point of no return has moved a little further up the age range. Most primary schools are no longer dominated by the need

1

to get as many of their 'bright' children as possible through a test which, as far as parents are concerned, will make or break them for life. Most 11-year-olds these days move up together to comprehensive secondary schools without having been separated into sheep and goats. Even so, secondary schools of all types, with honourable exceptions, are still struggling to break out of their apparently inherent capacity to demotivate an alarmingly high proportion of English and Welsh children. (Scotland, on the whole, has a more effective system.)

They are the 'bottom 40 per cent' that Sir Keith Joseph agonised over, and for whom there have, over the last three decades, been almost more prescriptions for success than there have been Ministers of Education: educational priority schools, the Certificate of Secondary Education, the Technical and Vocational Education Initiative, the Low Attaining Pupils Project, 'relevance', vocationalism, BTEC and City and Guilds initiatives, all have come and some have gone, yet so far there has been no significant rise in the performance of the least successful of our secondary-age pupils. Low expectation almost appears to be built into the system, and not just for the least able children.

The mid-1980s have seen an acceleration of new initiatives taken by the Conservative government, culminating in the introduction of the new GCSE examination and the passing of an Education Reform Act in 1988 which introduced a National Curriculum, additional assessment, and two new types of secondary school. This is just the latest attempt to raise standards of performance across the board in secondary schools, standards which, although they have in some respects improved dramatically over the last two decades, are pretty universally acknowledged to fall behind those of our industrial competitors. This book will attempt to look at why the most recent changes have been made, and to assess their chances of success, in the light both of the political controversy which still surrounds the implementation of major sections of the 1988 Act, and of the new shortage of qualified teachers.

But first, a little history. It is easily forgotten that for the majority of the British population over the age of 50 secondary education did not exist. Up to and during the Second World War the majority of children completed their education in the elementary-school system, many attending the same 'all-age' school from the age of 5 until they left at 14 to go straight into a job. In 1938 there were less than half a million children in genuine secondary schools – either grammar or technical – which provided examination courses up to the age of 16. And of that privileged minority, less than half received their secondary education free: the rest paid either full or partial fees.

Even before the war the political will was growing to introduce radical change in the education system for all children over the age of 11: but 50 years later it is at least arguable, certainly in England, that change has never been fully implemented and that the shadow of the rigidly stratified pre-war system of schooling still falls across much of what we now fondly regard as a system of genuine equal opportunity for all.

The 1944 Education Act, the 'Butler Act' as it came to be called after R. A. Butler, the Conservative minister who steered it through Parliament, was passed with all-party support even before the war ended. This was part of the radical reconstruction planned for British society, which was supposed to sweep away many of the inequalities of the 1930s. The Act was intended to bring about 'secondary education for all', a pre-war Labour Party slogan to which even Winston Churchill, not a noticeable egalitarian, was reluctantly converted. But in three important respects the Butler Act promised more than it could deliver.

In the period of frantic reconstruction under conditions of national near-bankruptcy which followed the war, far from gaining access as of right to 'secondary education' at the age of 11, as the Act promised, many young people in the 1940s still found themselves trapped in 'all-age' elementary schools, especially in rural areas. It was not until the early 1950s that the last senior elementary classes closed their doors.

Similarly the Act's promise to raise the school-leaving age to 16, so giving all children a realistic opportunity to sit a school-leaving examination, was indefinitely postponed, as was the even more ambitious provision for part-time education for all up to 18. At a time when there were not enough classrooms to accommodate all the children of the post-war baby boom and the first generation of prefabs was hastily being erected in school playgrounds, the post-war Labour government, to its credit, did raise the leaving age to 15. But it was not until 1972, after years of political and educational prevarication, that all children were finally required to remain at school until 16 for what had been regarded as the full term of a genuine secondary education almost since the foundation of the grammar schools.

But it was in its recommendations on the organisation of secondary education that the 1944 Act was most seriously deficient. Instead of legislating for a genuinely fresh start, it merely heralded what was at first a muted, but eventually became a passionate battle over the structure of secondary schooling. Almost 50 years later it is still the structure of the secondary system, with its division into well-funded and high-status grammar schools, and less well-funded and generally poorly regarded secondary moderns, which in some parts of England still militates against the highest quality of secondary education and genuine equality of opportunity for all children.

It is perhaps understandable that a wartime coalition should balk at prescribing root and branch reform. Going further than the Act did – and its wording on the structure of secondary education is ambiguous and allowed some experimentation even in the 1940s – would have had incalculable long-term costs for local and national government at a time when the extent of the post-war reconstruction required was becoming only too apparent. Education might have moved up the scale of political priorities during the war, but the rebuilding of factories and houses was always going to take priority over another wholesale reorganisation so soon after the abolition of the all-age elementary schools.

Even so, it is surprising that a coalition which included Labour Party ministers should have swallowed so completely the specious intellectual case which had been made by the Norwood Report, upon whose conclusions the 1944 Butler Act was based. Norwood concluded, conveniently enough for the public purse, that a system of secondary schools based on the existing selective grammar schools, where fee-paying would be abolished, the 'modern' schools which had begun to replace the senior classes of the elementary schools, and the handful of technical secondary schools which had been established by some local authorities, would meet the needs of the nation's children – who were assumed to fall neatly into the three categories of aptitude and ability that these three types of secondary school required. Norwood based his rationale for this tripartite system of secondary education on the work of psychologists who, throughout the 1920s and 1930s, had been attempting to perfect a means of measuring 'intelligence' and had concluded not only that such a human trait existed and was measurable but also that it was pretty well fixed at an early age for life. Hence the argument that a measurement taken at the age of 11, at the end of primary schooling, could quite legitimately and equitably be used as a justification for providing a particular kind of education for different groups of children, an education widely believed to be 'appropriate' to their abilities.

Even in 1943, *The Times Education Supplement* could see the inherent disadvantages of such a system. Though the tripartite system might be an advance on the pre-war system, they argued, 'it would remain true that modern schools will be places which all or many will try to avoid'. Even Sir Cyril Burt, upon whose work on intelligence much of the structure of selection at 11 was based, drew the line at Norwood's identification of three qualitatively different groups of children with 'different types of mind'.

This view entirely reverses the facts as they are now known to us. . . . The proposed allocation of all children to different types of school at the early age of eleven cannot provide a sound psychological solution ... the grounds are administrative rather than psychological.

Writing in 1952, when the full implications of what Norwood had proposed had become clear in one local authority area after another, the educational historian S. J. Curtis wrote:

> Seldom has a more unscientific or more unscholarly attitude disgraced the report of a public committee. The suggestion seems to be that the Almighty has benevolently created three types of child in just those proportions which would gratify educational administrators.

The introduction of a tripartite system of secondary education was not the last time that schools were reorganised as much for administrative and financial convenience as for educational reasons. Many a later comprehensive scheme of reorganisation hinged as much on the availability and convenience of school premises as upon any more exalted rationale. But the 1944 decision – spelt out more clearly in the parliamentary debate of the period than in the actual letter of the Act – made inevitable the debate over the structure of secondary schooling which still bedevils English education. It is instructive that a high proportion of the schools taking advantage of the 1988 Education Act's provisions for 'opting out' of local authority control and becoming semi-independent are from amongst the grammar schools which had their status confirmed by the post-1944 secondary reform and have somehow survived the subsequent grindingly slow 40 years of progress towards a 'common' or comprehensive secondary school for which some educationists and politicians were already arguing in the 1930s.

Of course the structure of secondary education does not in itself militate against high-quality education, although it has to be remembered that only 4 per cent of children ever made it into the third part of the tripartite system, the technical schools which local authorities proved extremely reluctant to provide, and that the secondary modern schools, excellent as some of them turned out to be, were invariably less well funded and resourced than the grammar schools. Yet the fact that the 1944 Act did not grasp the nettle of a divided, selective system did have its effect, directly and indirectly, on the quality of secondary education for several more generations of secondary-school children thereafter. Eighty per cent of 11-year-olds, under the tripartite system, moved into schools which were less well resourced, had less well-qualified teachers and could offer only a more limited academic curriculum and more limited access to public examinations. Yet an increasing number of these children, despite their supposed 'failure' at 11, soon began to prove their capabilities by staying at school at least until they were 16, if not older. The enormous increase in academic success amongst middle-ability children following the introduction of the CSE examination, and the more recent improvement in performance in the GCSE, shows how far 80 per cent of young people's abilities were underestimated by the rigid selective system. The loss of morale amongst some youngsters at 11, such as my own class in that south-west secondary modern school, can never, of course, be measured.

But there was more than that. Much political, teacher and parental energy was consumed over three decades as the autonomous English local authorities switched, area by area, school by school, to a comprehensive system of organisation (the Scots and Welsh, where the schools reflected class divisions less clearly, made the transition with far less political aggravation).

It was a war which started quietly enough, with many rural counties of all political persuasions making the change with little dissent from the electorate once an initial reluctance by Whitehall to approve reorganisation plans in the early 1950s had been overcome. Indeed it is often forgotten that early pressure for an end to the 11-plus test and the introduction of comprehensive schools came from middle-class parents who bitterly resented their children being consigned to what they regarded as second-class secondary modern schools.

By the 1970s, by which time a Labour government had

been pressing local authorities to make the change since 1965, it had become politically contentious, with the Conservative party increasingly supporting those few, mainly Conservative-controlled, local authorities who were standing out for the retention of grammar schools. Ironically, during her period as Secretary of State for Education, Margaret Thatcher found that she had little alternative but to approve more schemes of reorganisation than any of her predecessors. But the backlash had by then begun in earnest. The reform was being linked by some politicians of the Right, and increasingly in the media, with an alleged fall in secondary-school standards. By the end of the 1980s, comprehensive reorganisation in England is still incomplete, is still contentious, and is still distracting attention from some of the far more crucial issues which have also faced secondary education for twenty years or more.

This is by no means to argue that the structure of secondary education is unimportant or that comprehensive reform was not justified. It is still difficult to comprehend how an advanced country with an increasingly serious shortage of skilled workers, and one of the worst records in the industrialised world for keeping young people in education beyond the compulsory school age, can justify the perpetuation, even on a very limited scale, of a selection system which denies a majority of young people access to what their supporters claim the 'best' (i.e. grammar) schools can offer. We are not so effective in our schooling system, or so well endowed with talent, that we can afford to deter, demoralise or deny a single young person the fullest opportunity at the tender age of 11.

Until very recently, the battle for comprehensive education effectively appeared to be over. Almost 90 per cent of young people are now being taught in comprehensive schools. Attempts to reintroduce selection in some areas, such as Solihull and Milton Keynes, had been rejected by parents. But following the 1988 Act it remains to be seen whether the more oblique political assault on the comprehensive system launched through the introduction of City Technology Colleges and grant-maintained schools, and the proposed 'magnet' schools (see p. 39), will seriously undermine the system or merely fray it at the edges. What is obvious already is that there is even now no consensus in England (Scotland and Wales, one has to say again, are rather different) in favour of the common neighbourhood secondary school which attracts such strong community support in many other countries, including the United States. The shadow of a hierarchical system, neatly reflecting the English class structure, still falls heavily across English secondary education.

Yet while recognising that the structure of schooling is important in providing all young people with equal opportunities, it is with some of the other issues, which have tended to be overshadowed by the prolonged comprehensive political battles, that I intend to deal in this book. There are good schools and bad schools within any structure, and it is undoubtedly in the interests of young people and of the nation that we should maximise the number of good schools and reduce the number of the bad. But while many of the middle classes were fighting to preserve the grammar schools, good, bad and indifferent – and incidentally the privileged position of their own children – questions of measuring and of raising standards, of the need to modernise the curriculum and the examination system, of how to prepare young people for work and introduce them to technology, and of accountability to parents and the community tended to be overlooked.

Three factors eventually pushed some of these other issues to the fore. The first was the OPEC decision to raise oil prices in the early 1970s, an event which ended a period of expansion such as education had never before enjoyed. By 1976, when the Labour government began to cut public spending, the first complaints from parents and teachers reached newspapers like the *Guardian*, where I was then editing the first national newspaper education page, that schools were running short of books and other equipment. The party, in terms of relatively generous educational spending, was undoubtedly over, although as unemployment began to bite, the nation's need for an increasingly highly skilled output of school- and college-leavers to help regenerate British industry had never been more acute.

The second factor which concentrated minds on what was going on inside the secondary schools, rather than simply on how they were organised, was the rapid decline in the birth rate throughout the 1970s. Writing about education then, one was only too well aware that the primary schools were being decimated by the decline in the number of children. This decline began to hit the secondary schools, especially in the inner cities where there was population loss anyway, by the mid-1970s. A second, even more hard-fought round of school closures now began simply in response to the downturn in pupil numbers. But almost unbelievably it was not until the mid-1980s that British employers actually seemed to realise that the 'demographic time-bomb', as John Banham of the Confederation of British Industry called it, the fuse of which had been lit as far back as 1970, was about to hit them. Suddenly British school-leavers, whom it had so recently been safe to consign to schemes of very variable quality like YTS, were to be in such short supply that they would have to be wooed into jobs again.

The third factor to bring educational issues other than the comprehensive one to the fore was quite simply the election in 1979 of a Conservative government under a Prime Minister committed to a programme of radical change which, by the 1987 election, had got around to education. Suddenly, for a hectic two years, in the hands of an Education Secretary determined to make his political mark, secondary education – its structure, its content, the balance of control between central and local government, between parents and teachers, industry and the community – came under the almost daily scrutiny of Parliament, the media and a whole gamut of experts from the far Right, who, after years of being ignored by the educational 'establishment', felt that at last their various schemes for a free market in schooling would be listened to. Suddenly education ceased to be a political Cinderella and became the belle of the ball – although this was not, in the political circumstances, a position many educationists much appreciated once they had attained it. The attention was by no means the sort they had been seeking.

In the rest of this book I shall attempt to tease out the effects both of the long-term changes which have affected secondary schools since 1944, and the more recent, and radical switches of emphasis brought about by the Education Reform Act, which Kenneth Baker clearly hoped would eventually be compared historically with the Butler Act itself. But the lead times in education are slow. An Act passed tomorrow may take ten years to come to fruition in the schools. Many generations of secondary schoolchildren will pass through the system before it is possible to pass even an interim judgement on Mr Baker and his Bill.

Chapter 1
LOSS OF FAITH

It is difficult to know just when national disillusionment with secondary education set in, or indeed how deep it has ever really run outside the vivid imaginations of some newspaper leader writers and the pronouncements of some politicians. That there were political reasons for denigrating educational standards was apparent even as early as 1969 when the first of a series of critical pamphlets, the Black Papers, by mainly right-of-centre educationists began to attack the notion of comprehensive education as well as so-called 'progressive' teaching methods. If you wish to return to a highly regarded *status quo* (grammar schools and formal, didactic teaching, in the case of the Black Paper writers) or to introduce something radically new (intervention in the school curriculum in the case of James Callaghan's Labour government in 1976 or a fully nationalised curriculum and new types of schools, in the case of the 1987 Conservative government), it is in your interests to knock whatever is going on at present.

Throughout this period, though, when parents were given a direct say, as they are when a reorganisation scheme of some kind is being debated, their instinct seemed almost invariably to be to fight for preservation of what they already had, be it a grammar school or a comprehensive, a single-sex or a co-educational establishment or a sixth form. (Never forget the parents of Solihull who were offered their grammar schools back and declined because, although they might not object to grammar schools, they certainly did not want secondary moderns as well.) It is interesting to note that the first score or so of schools which have 'opted out' of local authority control as a result of the new Education Act are almost all schools with some distinctive attribute they wish to preserve: either they have grammar, single-sex or voluntary-aided status, or they are anxious not to see their sixth form reorganised away. The English are a highly conservative nation; the Welsh and the Scots have so far shown little interest in 'opting out'.

Politicians, both Labour and Conservative, have been becoming progressively more interested in radical educational change ever since the mid-1970s. And this time it has not been a change in the structure of secondary education that has concerned them, so much as a change in what goes on inside schools. And that, and particularly what had become known as the 'secret garden' of the curriculum, was the area which ever since the 1944 Education Act had been regarded as the preserve of the local education authorities and of the schools and teachers themselves, not of the ostensible senior partner in the education system, the Minister in Whitehall who, while he or she might command an enormous budget, had almost no control over how it was spent.

By the mid-1960s the media, particularly the right-of-centre national newspapers, had become deeply involved with the pro-grammar school, pro-'traditional standards' side of the comprehensive battle and were no slouches at depicting teachers as (favourite word) 'dunces' and schools as 'blackboard jungles', or at seeking out 'Red heads' or 'Lefty teachers', should the occasion demand. This was after all the period in which 'grammar school' became almost synonymous with 'good school' and 'comprehensive' with 'bad' in some parts of the media as the debate on secondary-school reorganisation increasingly became politicised and Conservative education authorities reluctant to reorganise became embattled with Labour administrations in Whitehall.

The newspapers lost the comprehensive war. But when new motives for knocking state schools were provided, firstly by the economically beleaguered Labour government from 1976 and then redoubled by Mrs Thatcher's right-wing radical advisers in the 1980s, the popular Press and some of what Bruce Kemble of the London *Evening Standard* dismisses as the 'unpopular papers' were not slow to oblige. 'Loony left' councils and their policies on racism and sexism soon became the target, and myths like 'Baa, Baa, green sheep', the anti-racist nursery rhyme that never was, were given wide credence.

As the 1970s progressed there emerged another, unspoken, government motive for running down what the secondary schools in particular were achieving. The economic recession which followed the oil crisis, and which was exacerbated by the industrial 'restructuring' of the early years of the Thatcher government, led inexorably to extremely high levels of youth unemployment throughout the early 1980s. It was much easier to blame the schools and young people themselves, with their alleged lack of basic and technological skills, for their desperate plight on the dole than to regard this as the result of economic circumstances at least partly under government control. So an economic crisis, which in fact made the job of secondary schools considerably harder as young people began to lose their faith in the usefulness of qualifications, came to be seen as an effect of young people's school failure rather than as a contributory cause of it.

The media, with a few exceptions, obliged where they could with evidence for an ill-disciplined and disintegrating school system where few school-leavers had apparently succeeded in learning to read and write – in spite of the fact that results in public examinations steadily improved throughout the period. A series of secondary schools – from Risinghill and Islington Green in London to Countesthorpe in Leicestershire and Madeley Court in Shropshire – found themselves at various times the unlucky focus of media interest in lax discipline, poor standards or 'progressive' methods. Most were later vindicated by Her Majesty's Inspectors or by their local authorities, but by then the reputation of the whole system had been further eroded.

Improving examination performance may explain why, in spite of media campaigns, opinion polls showed and still do show a consistently high level of support by parents for their own children's secondary schools, 80 per cent satisfaction not being unusual. Similar polls revealed a widespread public acknowledgement, even by non-parents, that children on the whole get a better education in modern schools than adults believe they received themselves a generation before. Parents' confidence in the schools they actually know appears to have remained remarkably high throughout the period of attack on state school standards in general and comprehensive school standards in particular by politicians and the media.

This retention of parental confidence may be partly due to the remarkable change of ethos in many secondary schools that resulted directly from the comprehensive reform programme which, even where it had begun slowly and cautiously, accelerated after the raising of the school-leaving age in 1972. Historically, the grammar schools had modelled themselves on the public schools: rules of dress were strictly enforced for neatly uniformed pupils and be-gowned staff alike, relationships between teachers and taught were formal, the school day and the timetable were tightly structured, discipline rigid and very often enforced by physical punishment. The secondary modern schools, however, with their sometimes less than compliant clientele and their necessarily less obsessive interest in public examinations, had in many cases pioneered a more informal approach to learning, with a strong emphasis on the pastoral care of pupils as well as teaching skills.

When schools of these two types were brought together in a comprehensive structure there were those which took the grammar-school road, particularly in the early days, and ran what was essentially a grammar school alongside a secondary modern under the same roof, and with all the benefits of the 'grammar-school tradition' for all. (Research later showed that such schools proved to be the least successful comprehensives, but that is another story.) Other new comprehensives followed a different road, emphasising the pastoral tradition of the secondary moderns, introducing a structure of year heads, form tutors or pastoral staff under some other title, whose main role was to ensure that young people of all abilities and aptitudes benefited from what the school had to offer and had someone to turn to immediately any difficulty arose. Many created a substantially more informal and relaxed atmosphere in which teachers and young people worked together rather than in opposition, and the cane, even if formally retained, was almost never used. Over time, that sort of management structure and school organisation – with heads of academic departments or faculties responsible for academic affairs and a parallel group of staff responsible for the care and supervision of the students – has become a standard feature of comprehensive schools. It is at least arguable that this staffing pattern – which should in theory facilitate communication between home and school during the difficult adolescent years – allied to a more relaxed and constructive relationship between teachers and students which is the hallmark of very many of the most successful comprehensive schools, has done a great deal to reassure parents about the quality and stability of their local school at a time of unprecedented change and uncertainty in education.

At the level of national politics, though, the 1970s and 1980s undoubtedly cannot fail to be remembered as the period of the great denigration of state education. The treatment of Shirley Williams's Green Paper, *Education in Schools*, in 1977 is instructive. This followed the speech by Prime Minister Callaghan at Ruskin College, Oxford, a year earlier which launched the so-called Great Debate on education, a series of meetings around the country between teachers, administrators, industrialists and others which sought to achieve a consensus on how to tackle the educational weaknesses identified by the Prime Minister. Mr Callaghan's message was essentially that although standards of education were rising slowly, a society in deep economic trouble in an increasingly competitive world needed to raise them even faster.

The Green Paper made pretty clear that educational standards had not fallen – even though Callaghan's speech had generally been taken by the media as an endorsement of exactly that position, the position many newspapers had been taking on their own initiative, and for deeply political reasons, for a number of years by 1977. The Green Paper took a different line, which most of the press duly ignored.

It is simply untrue that there has been a general decline in educational standards. Critics who argue on these lines often make false comparisons, for instance with some non-existent educational golden age, or by matching today's school-leavers against those of a generation ago without allowing for the fact that a far larger proportion of today's boys and girls stay on into the sixth form. [and so are not competing for jobs at 16]

Recent studies have shown clearly that today's school children read better than those of thirty years ago. Far more children, over a wider range of ability, study a modern language or science than did a generation ago. Many more take and pass public examinations. Many more go on to full-time higher education. (*Education in Schools*, 1977, para. 1.4)

From this temperate beginning, the Green Paper goes on to propose a national agreement on the curriculum, better assessment and record-keeping in schools, closer links between schools and industry, more attention during teacher training to the 'national importance of industry and commerce', to the preparation of pupils for life in a democratic and multi-cultural society, and an effort in the schools to end the sexual stereotyping which was hindering the progress of girls in certain subjects.

The Green Paper was greeted in almost all the national newspapers with glee. Headlines ranged from 'Sack the School Dunces' in the *Daily Express* to 'Weeding Out Incompetent Teachers' in *The Times*, by way of the *Daily Mail* which declared itself 'delighted that the things we have been saying for years are finally beginning to trickle through'. Only the *Guardian* reported more soberly that 'The Education Plan Avoids Conflict'. Not in the national Press it didn't!

Margaret Thatcher is said to believe that policy is essentially a matter of presentation. The presentation of a whole series of reports on British state schools in the national media has implied that the schools are failing, quite regardless of what the reports actually said. The consensus became not what Mr Callaghan, or the HMI report on secondary education in 1979, or indeed in 1988, actually said: that standards were actually rising but needed to rise more quickly, that the vast majority of schools were orderly places, but that some schools lacked resources, found it difficult to recruit teachers in some specialist areas, and that buildings were being allowed to fall into serious disrepair. The consensus became that standards had fallen, that teachers were often incompetent and could not be sacked, and that what one minister in 1986 contemptuously dismissed as the 'ed. biz' could safely be ignored when making educational policy.

And indeed the 'ed. biz' – which one might assume includes local authority administrators, the entire teaching profession and teacher educators, but which turned out to include representatives of parents' groups as well – was duly ignored when it came to the so-called 'consultation' on the 1987 Education Reform Bill, which became the 1988 Act.

As Julian Haviland so meticulously records in *'Take Care, Mr Baker!'* (Fourth Estate, 1988), his summary of the responses to the brief summer of debate which preceded the publication of the Bill, most of the reactions were carefully and thoughtfully worked out, and surprisingly seldom opposed to the principle of what much of the Bill was designed to achieve. There was as much emphasis on the sheer complexity and impracticability, and what might turn out to be the prohibitive cost, of what was proposed as on its undesirability. The exception was the case of grant-maintained schools and open enrolment, for which few people had a good word to say, regarding the introduction of a 'market' in schooling as an exercise which risked actually damaging the education of the significant number of children who would be left behind at the bottom of a new hierarchy of different kinds of schools. All that careful, well-meaning and well-informed comment could be safely ignored – indeed, it would not even have been published but for Mr Haviland – as the Bill went through Parliament virtually unscathed, mainly because the 'ed. biz' had been successfully traduced over a long period of time.

There is no doubt that the period of concerted attack upon state education has had other significant consequences for all schools, but perhaps particularly for secondary schools. There has been, for instance, a severe loss of confidence in state education amongst the middle classes. Writing in the *Independent*, Robert Chesshyre describes returning from America with his family to discover that he was closely questioned by friends and neighbours about what he was going to do with his children. He was, he says, 'deeply dismayed to find that almost everyone else living in our fairly modest outer London residential street avoided the school at the end of the road as if it were the seat of some sort of social plague, and packed off their children to private schools every morning by the Volvo-load'. His neighbours were part of the reversal in the fortunes of the private-school sector, where only a few years earlier I heard headteachers discussing gloomily at the Headmasters' Conference which of their number would have to close down over the next few years.

Mr Chesshyre sent his children to the local comprehensive school, where they thrived. He could, he argued, see no way in which any nation could aspire to be a thoroughgoing democracy if its more privileged citizens educated their offspring in an exclusive system. That was not a view much heard publicly by the end of the 1980s, by which time public confidence in the maintained system of education had reached a low ebb.

It would, of course, be foolish to deny that there were not real problems in the state school system throughout the 1970s and 1980s, particularly in some inner-city areas. HMI reports confirmed what parents were saying: that in some comprehensive schools, ostensibly established to provide equal opportunities for all, expectations of what children could do remained far too low. The Hargreaves Report on inner London schools, commissioned by the Inner London Education Authority, came to the same conclusion and proposed some radical remedies for raising standards.

But this does not mean that those problems were not consistently exaggerated, manipulated, and in some cases exacerbated throughout the period for political ends. As Secretary of State for Education, Sir Keith Joseph, a kindly and almost agonisingly thoughtful man, did much to reduce the morale of the teaching profession to its lowest ebb for decades, partly by his rigid insistence on a monetarist approach to economic policy which meant that teachers' pay had to be held down at all costs, and partly by his public and demoralising worrying over the defects of the system in general and the profession in particular. He was removed from office to the House of Lords after the schools had suffered two years of industrial action, and all the progress which could have been made towards raising standards of achievement through his White Paper, *Better Schools*, and the introduction of the GCSE examination, both of which were widely welcomed, had degenerated into recrimination.

Whether the demolition of public confidence in the state education system in the time of Sir Keith Joseph was intentional or accidental may be a subject of endless political debate. He was working on a structure which had already been seriously weakened. The fact remains that by the end of his tenure of office in 1986, public confidence was low, the flight of the middle classes to the private sector, especially in London, had begun, and the teaching profession was embittered. Kenneth Baker completed teachers' humiliation by taking away their negotiating rights and imposing a pay settlement and a new contract which had the positive effect of getting them back to normal working, but without resolving any of their long-standing grievances. Recruitment to teacher-training courses fell, and the first signs of a serious teacher shortage began to emerge.

What the Conservative Party proposed by way of educational reform – a reform which involved a massive centralisation of control over the curriculum and examination system allied to a weakening of local authority control over individual schools – was published as a Bill in the autumn of that year, and received the Royal Assent, having been modified only marginally by Parliament, in July 1988.

If political scientists need a casebook example of politics by presentation they could do worse than examine what happened to state education in Britain between James Callaghan's speech about raising school standards in 1976 and the passing of the Education Reform Act in 1988. What had begun as a genuine enough attempt to bring British education more closely into line with the needs of a post-industrial economy ended with a series of measures which, at least potentially, opened the way for the eventual privatisation of state education through the fragmentation of the local authority system, and put in place a structure for controlling what is taught in the schools which could potentially be used for any political end whatsoever.

Chapter 2

THE STATE OF THE SECONDARY SCHOOLS

For an objective view of what has happened to secondary education over the last decade, we rely on three main sources of information: statistics collected by national government and the local authorities, reports by the local authorities themselves and by independent organisations like the National Confederation of Parent–Teacher Associations and the Campaign for the Advancement of State Education, and reports from Her Majesty's Inspectors. The latter are a body of independent professionals, recruited in the main from the schools or educational administration. They are not civil servants, although they report to the Secretary of State on the condition and performance of the schools and public-sector colleges (though not the universities).

Statistics give a stark outline of what has happened to the secondary sector over the last decade. Between 1979 and 1988 the number of pupils fell by no less than 20.7 per cent and the decline is expected to continue until at least 1992 before pupil numbers begin to rise slowly again. Not surprisingly, the number of secondary schools has also fallen. No less than 540, 11.5 per cent, of maintained secondary schools have closed their doors for ever over the last ten years, which is not nearly as many as both ministers and independent bodies such as the Audit Commission believe should have closed in order to make the most economic use of secondary-school facilities. But parents almost always fight school closures fiercely and the process is fraught with political difficulties for local authorities, quite apart from the erratic nature of decisions taken by successive Ministers of Education, who have the final say over closures and amalgamations. As a result, many secondary schools have simply been reduced in size over the last ten years, leaving some in considerable difficulties as they struggle to provide a full curriculum, particularly for students over 16, with a decreasing number of teachers and diminishing resources.

Even so, the reduction in the number of secondary schools has been inexorable and the private sector has not escaped completely. Independent schools have closed too, with numbers down by more than 80 over the same ten-year period to 1986, although in this sector pupil numbers have actually risen. The percentage of the total school population attending independent schools was 7.1 in 1988, compared with 5.8 per cent in 1979, and independent school heads were talking bullishly about raising the proportion to 10 per cent by the end of the decade.

In spite of all the disruption caused by rationalisation, the examination qualifications of school-leavers continued to improve throughout most of the period. While the number of young people gaining at least five O levels (or the equivalent-grade CSE) rose from 22.8 per cent to 26.7 per cent between 1976 and 1986, the number of young people leaving school without any GCE or CSE qualification at all dropped from 16.7 per cent to under 10 per cent. Although statistics about the performance of the whole age-group will not be available for some time, it appears that the first two years of the new GCSE examination have improved the performance of young people at 16 even further. The proportion of young people gaining two passes at A level, the minimum entrance qualification for a degree course, has improved more slowly and began to level out in the mid-1980s at around 13 per cent.

The proportion of young people staying in education beyond the minimum school-leaving age of 16 is another measure of how successful secondary schools have been, and in this area British performance notoriously lags behind that of many other industrialised countries. Again, after a steady rise over a number of years in the proportion of young people staying at school beyond 16, the statistics show a decline after 1982 from a peak of 34 per cent. Even allowing for the fact that an increasing number of school sixth forms have been replaced by tertiary colleges, which generally prove very attractive to 16-year-olds, and that the further education colleges had a relatively successful decade in attracting school-leavers to full-time courses, the full-time staying-on rate in schools and colleges together hit a peak of 47.4 per cent in 1982 and then went into a slow decline. It reached 47 per cent again, according to provisional figures, only in 1988. There are also sharp discrepancies between local authorities. Under 20 per cent of 16-year-olds stayed at school in Barnsley, less than half the rate in Surrey, Barnet and Brent, reflecting a sharp variation between the north and the south-east of England averages. The introduction of the GCSE examination does appear to be encouraging more young people to stay in education beyond 16, but with only two years' results available it is still too early to say whether this trend will be a permanent result of a reform which is generally regarded as more motivating for young people than the dual O-level/CSE examination system which preceded it. The fact remains that in international comparisons, Britain keeps an unusually low proportion of its young people in full-time education beyond 16, and compares even less well internationally when those staying on until 18 – just over 30 per cent – are taken into account. In the United States it is the norm for young people to remain in high school beyond 16, and 71.8 per cent of the age-group graduate at 18. In Japan 94.1 per cent stay in education until the age of 18, and in France 33 per cent gain the *baccalauréat*, the rough equivalent of A levels and the entry qualification for degree courses. The French Ministry of Education is introducing reforms which aim to increase the proportion gaining the '*bac*' to 70 per cent of the 18-year-old age-group. Of the most advanced industrial countries, only West Germany keeps a similarly low proportion of young people in education to 18 – 29 per cent – and that country backs up its school system with a highly developed system of vocational and technical education to provide training for most young workers.

Spending patterns for education in the same period are more difficult to interpret. The Callaghan government announced in the mid-1970s that the party was over as far as local government spending was concerned. Education gobbles up more than half of local government expenditure, and so was bound to be hard hit by any economies. Parents soon began to notice the effect of government policies in some areas and Shirley Williams, then the Labour government's Secretary of State for Education, was inundated with complaints about the inadequate supply of school books and equipment, and the deteriorating condition of school premises.

The Conservative government elected in 1979 was committed to cutting public expenditure even further and over the following seven years introduced various financial measures intended to persuade those local authorities, generally Labour-controlled, which were reluctant to cut back, to do so. By 1985 *The Times Educational Supplement* was reporting that cash penalties had forced four out of five LEAs to plan real cuts in their education budgets. Debates over rate-capping, the reduction in LEA grants from central government – to nil in the case of the Inner London Education Authority – and 'overspending' councils dominated the headlines in the educational press.

The paradox of the period was that although parents and teachers in the schools were acutely conscious of cuts, an analysis of government spending showed that even in the period before Kenneth Baker went to the DES and eased up slightly on school spending restraint, the 'cuts' were more cosmetic than real. As Stuart Maclure and Tony Travers pointed out in an analysis in *The Times Educational Supplement* (8 February 1985), educational spending had gone up in cash terms, even allowing for inflation. By 1989, spending on secondary education was 10 per cent higher in real terms than it had been in 1979.

Maclure and Travers's conclusion was that parents and teachers, and HMI, who went to considerable lengths to look at the state of the schools in the light of public expenditure restraint throughout the 1980s, were not imagining their privation. The fact was simply that cuts turned out to be highly differential. Local authorities controlled by Labour, or the centre parties, generally contrived to maintain fairly generous levels of funding until well into the late 1980s. Conservative authorities, including many in the rural shires, began to cut back from an already low base from 1976 onwards. By the mid-1980s the differential between high- and low-spending authorities was widening fast, and many action groups of parents in the low-spending areas were revealing themselves as very unhappy indeed – undoubtedly a factor in the loss of control by the Conservatives of a number of shire counties in the 1985 local elections.

Spending cuts were differential in another respect. Between 1979 and 1985 capital spending on schools fell by 50 per cent, and there were substantial cuts in other sectors such as school meals and transport. At the same time, spending on nursery education rose by almost 20 per cent, and spending on secondary education also rose, although not nearly so substantially. However by 1987–89, there had been a rise in real terms of £613 million a year in secondary-school spending, largely as a result of two years of exceptional generosity in 1987 and 1988 prompted by the introduction of GCSE and the impending National Curriculum. After that, secondary spending was projected to fall back again slightly, and this projection was made before the expected fierce attempts by the Treasury to cut educational spending hard in the 1989 settlement.

But however spending actually went, in many areas of the country there was a deep-seated conviction that levels of provision were deteriorating. Specific areas of concern in secondary schools were the dilapidation of buildings and the low, and in some cases diminishing, amount of money available for school books and equipment. Anyone who visits schools regularly can see that in some parts of the country – both in rural or semi-rural counties and in inner-city areas – the combination of ageing buildings and a decreasing amount of ready cash for rebuilding or general decoration and maintenance has led to some secondary schools declining to a sorry state. Sir Keith Joseph himself admitted in 1984 that some children were being taught in 'crummy' conditions, although he added that this did not necessarily preclude their gaining a good education.

The DES's own *Survey of School Buildings* in 1987 revealed that while some secondary schools had surplus space because of the effect of population decline, 17 per cent were still overcrowded and 36 per cent were housing pupils in those ubiquitous 'temporary' buildings which so disfigure school sites and whose temporary life seems to extend for anything up to 30 years.

The DES asked local authorities to estimate how much capital funding was needed to bring their schools up to standard. For secondary schools the total, and admittedly rough, estimate was up to £670 million to meet statutory and structural requirements, and up to a further £670 million to make desirable improvements to meet curriculum needs, special educational needs and much else. The local authority capital spending programme for 1988–89 was £369 million, a sum which covers all new building and improvements right through from nursery education to colleges run by the local authorities. A mere £55 million was specially earmarked by Kenneth Baker for improvements to tackle the problems identified in the *Survey of School Buildings*.

Some measure of the shortfall in capital spending needed to bring secondary schools up to the standards required for the 1990s can be gained by the level of expenditure being offered to upgrade existing school buildings which are to be converted into City Technology Colleges (CTCs). Capital spending on the first ten CTCs, only two of which will be in completely new buildings, totalled more than £77 million, £59.9 million of that from government funds. The two Haberdashers' Aske's Schools in south London were offered a £4 million government grant as an inducement to become a CTC, while the Kingshurst CTC in Solihull, housed in a former LEA secondary school, spent no less than £3.45 million on adaptation and refurbishment plus generous gifts of laboratories and equipment from industry before it opened its doors in 1988. At much the same time as the Solihull CTC was inviting the Press to look at its lavish new facilities, Mr

Baker announced 'a shot in the arm' for inner-city schools – an extra allocation of £10 million which would allow 40 local authorities to upgrade 350 schools and colleges – an average of £28,500 per improvement.

The other area where there has been constant statistical dispute over the last ten years is the pupil–teacher ratio. According to DES statistics, the pupil–teacher ratio (PTR) in English secondary schools improved from 16.7 pupils per teacher to 15.4 in 1988. (In independent schools, incidentally, the ratio had reduced to 11.3 pupils per teacher by then.) But this improvement is distorted by two factors. Again, there are sharp discrepancies in the PTRs provided by different local authorities, with urban authorities, understandably in view of their concentration of social problems, being generally more generous than those in rural areas. In 1987, for instance, the secondary PTR varied from under 12:1 in several London boroughs, to more than 17:1 in several southern English counties.

There may also be quite sharp discrepancies between the PTRs in different schools in the same local authority area owing to the effect of curriculum protection policies in small secondary schools. These ensure that schools which become too small to justify a full range of specialist staff at the standard PTR are allocated extra teachers so that subjects are not lost from the timetable. In their survey of secondary education published in 1989, HMI found that an overall PTR of 16.3:1 concealed a low of 14.8:1 in schools with less than 600 pupils which ran a sixth form, and a high of 17.6:1 in schools of more than 900 pupils without a sixth form.

These two factors may go some way to explaining why, when ministers congratulate themselves on an improving pupil–teacher ratio, many parents are less than convinced by the evidence of their own experience. Their school may be one of those which has not benefited much, if at all, from an average improvement which conceals wide discrepancies.

Statistics, in any case, can only give an impression of what has been happening to secondary schools in the early to mid-1980s: cuts, dwindling pupil numbers, closures and amalgamations, and levels of performance, as measured by exam results and staying-on rates, which had either stabilised or begun to fall back slightly by 1986.

For many parents, the more subjective picture was one of considerable turmoil. For every cut in services, or closure and amalgamation of a secondary school, there was often a fierce local battle to preserve the *status quo*. Ironically, in view of the level of media condemnation it suffered throughout the period, it was the Inner London Education Authority which, in a series of consultations, best succeeded in reducing its number of secondary schools. It managed to avoid the destructive battles with the local authority politicians and administrators on one side and parents, governors and teachers on the other that erupted in so many other places.

But declining school rolls, closures and amalgamations with the redeployment of staff which inevitably follows, do little for teacher morale. Nor do bitter disputes over pay and conditions which were what afflicted the schools in the mid-1980s, leading to the most prolonged period of industrial action by the teacher unions which the schools had ever seen, and ultimately the removal of teachers' negotiating rights – still not restored at the time of writing – and a series of governmentally imposed pay settlements and a new contract for school staff.

For a fuller picture of what has been going on in secondary schools over the last ten years, it is instructive to look at the two major surveys conducted by HMI in that time – *Aspects of Secondary Education in England* (HMSO, 1979) and *Secondary Schools, an Appraisal by HMI* (HMSO, 1981). The documents are not wholly comparable, because the earlier study concentrated on the fourth and fifth years of secondary education, but there is sufficient overlap to make a detailed comparison of the two well worth while.

The first point both surveys make is that most maintained secondary schools are orderly communities where staff and children are hard-working and there is little serious disruption. Even in 1979, at the height of public hysteria about indiscipline in schools, HMI found that only a very small minority of schools felt that they themselves were facing serious behavioural problems. By 1989, HMI had concluded that in 90 per cent of secondary schools the approach to discipline was based on clear guidelines and worked well: only 5 per cent were judged to be over-permissive in their approach, and another 5 per cent were regarded as too authoritarian, with an obsession with rules which built up resentment amongst pupils.

On resource questions, HMI tend to lend support to those many parents' groups and teachers' organisations who have argued long and hard that secondary education is underfunded. Provision of books, the 1989 report said, was good in only 10 per cent of schools; it was actually inadequate in a third. More than half of the schools studied were judged to have inadequate library provision, and in some cases HMI regarded it as doubtful whether the library was adequate to meet GCSE needs. And although the provision of equipment was found to be satisfactory in most schools, and the provision of microcomputers appeared to be improving, these were often not linked to the general curriculum but confined to information technology lessons or classrooms.

HMI also confirmed the other major concern of parents, reflected in more informal surveys by parents' organisations: the poor state of many school buildings. Half the schools, they reported, were poorly decorated and in nearly a third the general maintenance was poor. During their inspection, in one 11-to-16 comprehensive school five out of seven science laboratories were out of use because of dry rot, and in another there was a 'general air of depression' caused by broken windows, poor plasterwork, a leaking roof and old classroom furniture.

As far as a more subjective judgement of a decade of change is concerned, the HMI surveys reveal a slow but erratic improvement in standards of work, and a steady drift in the direction of a common curriculum for all pupils up to the age of 16, something now enshrined in law through the introduction of the National Curriculum. The teaching force had aged over the ten years, but although it was better qualified in

1989 than in 1979, few schools seemed to have developed a coherent policy for staff development, a worrying weakness at a time of increasingly rapid change and the devolution of extra responsibilities from the LEAs to the schools. And, unsurprisingly, by 1989 the inspectors found that the work of some schools was being affected by shortages of teachers in maths, science and technology.

More time was being spent on helping secondary pupils with special needs, with a gradual move away from withdrawing pupils from normal classrooms in favour of having special needs staff working alongside pupils in difficulties in the normal classroom setting. Overall, HMI felt that schools were catering least well for pupils of just below average ability.

To get a more detailed picture of the state of secondary schools it is necessary to focus a little closer. Two local authorities – Cheshire and the Inner London Education Authority – undertook major surveys of all their schools during the 1980s; the London report, *Improving Secondary Schools* (better known as the Hargreaves Report; ILEA, 1984), has become something of a national guide to the challenge of raising secondary schools' standards.

Cheshire Education Observed (Cheshire County Council, 1987) was the less policy-oriented of the two reports: its sub-title was *Celebrations and Concerns*, in that order, and much of the report does celebrate the achievements of the county's secondary schools. But it also highlights areas of concern and presents something of a microcosm of the national scene.

> The overwhelming impression is that despite Herculean individual efforts by most schools, their interior decoration is shabby and depressing. . . . We were assailed time and time again by governors, heads and staff that 'the County hasn't decorated for ten years or more', and, even worse, in many cases had never made good after repairs to electrical installations, damp damage from leaking roofs and so on. In one school we saw holes left after high alumina cement probing, which had remained since 1975! [This was in 1986!] In another school the huts which provided the accommodation for special needs pupils had holes in the floor, as had the French rooms in another.

31

The catalogue is a familiar one, particularly in the low-spending shire counties, although dilapidated schools are well known in some city areas too. The long-term damage is not merely to the fabric of publicly owned buildings, but also to the morale of those who have to work and play in them. As the Cheshire report puts it: 'Self-respecting people prefer to live and work in surroundings which enhance their self-respect. School-children treat the environment and buildings in which they live and function with respect and care if they are well maintained and well designed.'

In spite of these urgent difficulties, the Cheshire survey concluded that if there was one area of priority to which the county's education committee ought to address itself, it was the 'grave underfunding' of pupil–teacher ratios and teacher supply in the secondary schools. Every school in the county which was visited regarded the improvement of the pupil–teacher ratio as the most pressing problem at a time when the schools were attempting, almost simultaneously, to introduce new teaching methods, the GCSE examination and the government's other secondary-school initiative, the Technical and Vocational Education Initiative.

The report on inner London schools of the committee chaired by Professor David Hargreaves (then chief inspector of ILEA) concentrated on rather different issues. Its brief was to uncover ways of raising performance in secondary schools which were, and still are, by national standards relatively well provided for in terms of physical conditions and staffing. The Hargreaves Report, in other words, faced head-on the problem of underachievement and disaffection in urban schools, a problem we will return to later in this book.

At the end of the decade, secondary schools, it is clear, were places of mixed fortunes. They faced the challenges of the 1988 Education Act, to be implemented in the early 1990s, carrying with them a burden of previous change – some of it welcome and some not. Some had recovered neither the enthusiasm of staff nor the full range of activities which had been common before the teachers' industrial action. Having had a contract imposed by central government, some teachers were determined to work to that contract and offer not a second of their time more. Resentments undoubtedly lingered in many staffrooms as teachers saw the restoration of their negotiating rights postponed until 1991.

Structural change still threatened many secondary schools as pupil rolls continued to fall, although such change was complicated from 1989 by the option parents were offered by the 1988 Act to remove their school from local authority control. But even where neither opted-out schools nor the new breed of CTCs were added to the state education mix, local management of schools and open enrolment promised an increased level of competition between schools which might previously have seen themselves as complementary in a town or neighbourhood rather than as rivals for pupils and resources.

The conviction remained amongst teachers and parents in many areas, and was confirmed clearly enough by official reports, that whether or not the government had experienced a change of heart over some aspects of secondary-school funding, the system was and looked likely to remain seriously underfunded and short of crucial specialist staff if it was to meet the challenge of educating young people adequately for the 1990s.

A survey in the summer of 1989, just when the provisions of the 1988 Education Act were beginning to bite, revealed that as many as a third of teachers would like to leave the profession if the opportunity arose. For most teachers, of course, the opportunity does not arise. But many parental hearts must have sunk at the news that as many as one in three of their children's teachers would rather not be in the classroom or laboratory or workshop where they are currently teaching. It was not a good omen for secondary schools at the very beginning of a period of unprecedented innovation in the schools.

Chapter 3
COMPETE OR DIE

Local education authorities could be forgiven for being taken by surprise at the drop in primary pupil numbers during the 1970s. A fall in the birth rate which began slowly in 1970 became a catastrophic drop of about a third by the end of the decade, leaving many primary schools dangerously short of pupils. It could have been a unique opportunity to reduce class sizes, but financial restraints were too tight for that. But with the very long lead times needed to reorganise school systems, the four years from the birth of a child to that child's likely arrival at school as a 'rising-five' is administratively very short.

There is far less excuse for local authorities which failed to anticipate the drop in numbers in secondary education. That could be firmly predicted as children entered primary school seven years before transfer to the secondary sector. Even so, the reduction in the number of secondary schools has never kept pace with the fall in the number of children requiring secondary education. The consequences of that failure to plan the system adequately, when resources were stretched, which was mainly a political failure at local and sometimes also at national level, were financial and qualitative. If a budget, which many would argue is inadequate anyway, is spread more thinly across institutions, the quality of what each institution can offer is inevitably adversely affected.

This is not an argument that parents find easy to accept. There has always been parental resistance to very large secondary schools ever since comprehensive reorganisation greatly increased the average size of schools in order to ensure that they were large enough to sustain adequate sixth forms. There is little evidence, in fact, that large schools do students any harm provided that they are well run, whatever the parental perception. Some of the most prestigious private schools such as Eton and the Manchester and Bradford Grammar Schools have around 1,000 students each.

What is irrefutable is that very small secondary schools are very expensive to maintain if they are to offer a full curriculum both pre- and post-16. As numbers fall the justification for the full-time employment of the full range of specialist teachers is reduced. They cannot be provided with a full timetable, but it is not always possible to find part-time staff to fill the gaps. Nor can teachers always be redeployed as and when required.

Given unlimited funds, and no shortages of secondary specialist staff in subjects like maths and science, this would not matter. Small secondary schools could simply be more generously staffed so that they could cover the full curriculum. But given the extremely tight funding of local authorities over the last decade, and the growing shortage of teachers in some specialist areas, the subsidy of small schools has inevitably been undertaken at the expense of larger schools – hence the difference in pupil–teacher ratios between small schools and large schools pointed out by HMI in their 1988 survey (see p. 28). And hence the exhortations of both government and independent bodies such as the Audit Commission, which monitors local government spending, to local authorities to rationalise their school places as urgently as possible as pupil numbers fell.

Government advice on the optimum size for a secondary school has been consistent, although the decisions of ministers on individual school closure proposals certainly have not. The 1985 White Paper, *Better Schools*, suggested that 11-to-16 comprehensive schools should not be smaller than five forms of entry – at 30 pupils per class, a total size of 750 students under 16. This was a slight reduction on the previous recommendation of six forms of entry, 900 under-16s. The DES was consistent on numbers when it launched the City Technology College programme: it was recommended that CTCs should cater for between 750 and 1,000 students.

But this simple equation is complicated by the fact that

the DES also recommends that secondary schools should be able to sustain a sixth form of 150 students if they are to offer a full range of subjects to students over 16, something which many schools with intakes as low as 150 or 180 a year find it extremely difficult to do in areas where staying-on rates are low. The implication of this is that many secondary schools should have considerably more than 750 students under 16 to sustain an adequate sixth form. The alternative suggested by the DES is that schools should co-operate with each other post-16, an arrangement which parents have not always welcomed or found satisfactory. The alternative favoured by many local authorities, faced with catastrophically declining sixth-form numbers, has been to provide for the over-16s in separate sixth-form or tertiary colleges.

The attitude of Secretaries of State for Education to their own advice on secondary-school size has been highly ambivalent. Successive Secretaries have turned down closure or amalgamation proposals for secondary comprehensive schools with as few as 300 pupils. Most recently, both Kenneth Baker and John MacGregor have approved applications for grant-maintained status from comprehensives with as few as 500 pupils. (Grammar schools, with a restricted ability range and high staying-on rates, have always been viable with lower numbers.)

The fall in the number of secondary schools shows that rationalisation has been undertaken with some vigour, and in some areas it has been achieved with the co-operation of parents and governors, who have come to terms with the stark fact of declining recruitment. In other areas there has been fierce resistance to closure and amalgamation plans and a glimpse of the sort of 'market' in school places which is to become more common as the provisions of the 1988 Act come into effect.

In future the market will play a much greater role in deciding which schools close and which remain open: that is government policy as enshrined in the 1988 Act. Before that, local authorities had the right, when pupil numbers were falling, to attempt to spread pupils around the available schools to ensure that as many schools as possible remained educationally viable and did not require heavy subsidies to keep going. They did this by imposing planned admission limits (PALs), entry limits which could be below the actual physical capacity of the school. In other words, a school capable of accepting 210 first-year children might be restricted to 180 for a year so that its neighbour along the road did not fall below 180. The provision sounds far more draconian in theory than it ever was in practice. In most local authority areas well over 95 per cent of families gained places in their first choice of school. But where PALs did cause trouble, as they did in the small Yorkshire town of Dewsbury in 1987, the trouble could be very bitter indeed. Parents who had been encouraged by all political parties to expect some choice over where their children went to school felt extremely aggrieved to be deprived of the place they wanted by what they regarded as an administrative manoeuvre. In Dewsbury parents were prepared to keep their children out of school for a year, and take their battle to the High Court, to prove their point. Secondary transfer had for years been providing similar cases of parental intransigence – or determination, depending on one's point of view; these were usually resolved as vacancies occurred in the oversubscribed school and children could be admitted.

Planned admission limits, such as those Kirklees council tried to impose in Dewsbury, were killed off by the 1988 Act. From 1989, admissions to secondary schools will be by a new system of 'open enrolment' which means that a school must recruit up to its full physical capacity if it has applicants to fill the places. In many areas this will make little difference to recruitment patterns. Popular schools which were full in 1988 will still be full in 1989 and may have to turn some applicants away, using exactly the same sort of criteria as they used previously: how far children live from the school, whether they have brothers and sisters there, and so on. Where the number of children seeking places and the number of places available is roughly in balance, there will be little change.

But where local authorities have a surplus of places, there will no longer be any protection for schools which have difficulty in recruiting. Their numbers will fall, at a time when the local authority's ability to protect the curriculum in small schools is likely to be severely constrained by other aspects of the 1988 Act which concern the funding of schools. Inevitably some will decline to the point at which they have to seek their own closure.

Anyone who has lived through the prolonged agony of a reorganisation scheme fought hard and bitterly at local level and then turned down by the Secretary of State, might be forgiven for thinking that the 'market' might provide an equally equitable and certainly quicker way of removing surplus schools than the existing bureaucratic system. Stuart Sexton, a former Conservative political adviser at the DES, says that closure by market forces will remove from ministers the almost impossible task of weighing up fairly the two sides of the argument in closure battles. It will certainly remove some of the political opprobrium heaped upon politicians involved in closure decisions both locally and nationally.

However, what the introduction of a free market in secondary-school places also does is take away from the local authority any ability to plan the secondary-school system coherently for the next decade. Secondary-school numbers will continue to fall until 1992, and will then begin to rise slowly. Some places that will lie empty for the next two or three years will be needed in future. Planned admission limits gave LEAs the opportunity of preserving some of these at minimum expense for the duration of the 'trough' in numbers.

That ability to hold some school places in reserve, as it were, until numbers rise again will be made even harder by the financial provisions of the 1988 Act. This provides for schools to be funded according to a formula: 75 per cent of their budgets in future will be determined by the number and age of the pupils on roll. There will be some scope for the protection of small schools, but in many areas far less than was normal in the past.

So the squeeze on small secondary schools will be twofold.

They will not be able to maintain their pupil numbers, which are the basis of an adequate curriculum, or to compensate for low numbers by financial subsidy to provide extra teachers. The decline in the quality of education on offer in such schools will inevitably accelerate, with a detrimental effect both on their pupils and on recruitment from year to year.

At the same time, the fierceness of the market is being increased by other government policies. The introduction of grant-maintained schools – many of them schools which have voted to 'opt out' to escape the consequences of reorganisation – and of City Technology Colleges, more generously funded by the government and industry than comparable local authority schools, will increase the competition for first-year pupils and for sixth-formers. So will the possible incorporation into the maintained system of religious schools currently outside it. Some Muslim and Jewish schools which are at present run privately are anxious to gain voluntary-aided status, which allows for state funding while leaving the religious authorities some control. They claim the right to the same treatment as that accorded to many Roman Catholic and Church of England schools under the 1944 Education Act. So far no decision has been made on any such application by the DES, but one cannot be long delayed.

Elsewhere local authorities themselves are looking at policies which will increase rather than lessen the competition between secondary schools. One such policy, considered first in the London Borough of Wandsworth and then in Bradford, is to turn some secondary schools into 'magnets' on the American model. The theory is that some secondary schools will specialise in certain aspects of the curriculum – science, technology, languages or the arts – so attracting more motivated students and raising standards.

There is plenty of evidence that a few inner-city schools in the United States have managed to boost both recruitment and the motivation of pupils in deprived areas by specialising in this way. Kenneth Baker, who visited New York as Secretary of State for Education in 1988, made much of the apparent success of magnet schools on his return to England.

What he failed to mention, or perhaps was not told on his visit, was that schools around a 'magnet' soon experience greater difficulty in recruiting, and greater problems over motivation and discipline, as more able and motivated pupils are sucked away by their prestigious neighbour. It is on these grounds that opposition to the magnet principle has been fierce in this country: headteachers and governors in Wandsworth rejected the proposal even though it would have applied to all schools in the borough and brought extra funding. Reservations centred on the likelihood that a 'pecking order' would very soon develop, with schools specialising in 'academic' subjects like science and languages at the top, and those in vocational and practical areas of study at the bottom. It was also felt that specialisation by choice at the age of 13 or 14 was not desirable, especially at a time when a National Curriculum was being introduced which was supposed to ensure that all children studied a broad curriculum until they were 16. Magnet schools were also suspected of being a way of reintroducing selection to a comprehensive system, something which will be considered in greater detail in the next chapter.

However reluctantly, headteachers and governors have to some extent begun to come to terms with the fact that in future they will have to compete with their neighbours. The alternative, in any area where there are surplus secondary-school places, is falling recruitment and the ultimate threat of closure. Training courses for headteachers have begun to tackle areas of activity which were previously regarded as the prerogative of the business world. Marketing, public relations and the promotion of a school's 'image' to its customers, who are variously defined as parents, the community and/or industrial and commercial employers who are going to take on school-leavers, have become familiar if not commonplace at governors' and school staff meetings.

Undoubtedly many headteachers feel a deep unease about this approach. They resent not only the dehumanising language of industry, with well-educated young people actually on occasion being designated 'the product', but also the radical change in their own role from educational and academic leader to plant manager, which is the almost inevitable result of many aspects of the 1988 Education Act. Not least they resent the increasing inter-school competition inherent in the open enrolment proposals: very few heads appear to want their school to flourish at the direct expense of their neighbours.

However there is no doubt that while the open enrolment provisions of the 1988 Act remain in force and there are surplus school places, competition between secondary schools is inevitable. It is equally certain that if the penalty for failing to recruit pupils is ultimately the closure of the school, heads and governors will, however reluctantly, do their best to 'sell' their product to local parents, using whatever weapons are to hand: examination results of course, but also the excellence of their glossy brochures, the quality of their buildings, their drama productions or their sport.

None of this can be good news for small schools, or schools which decline in size over the next few years, or for the children in them. Schools under pressure will find themselves handicapped in the recruitment battle by declining resources as the funding follows the children into the most popular establishments. Parents are left with the dilemma of trying to decide just how far the popularity of a school mirrors genuine quality and effectiveness, and how far it merely reflects fashion or even prejudice: does quality mean more than a smart uniform, for instance, and how far does unpopularity reflect the reluctance of some parents to have their children attend schools with a significant proportion of children from a different racial or social group? And society as a whole is left to judge ultimately whether there is real foundation for the belief of the political Right that market forces in education can genuinely raise standards, or whether a system which sets school against school may not produce at least as many losers as winners, the losers being the children whose parents may have imagined that a state education system, funded by the taxpayer, guaranteed equality of opportunity and provision for all.

Chapter 4
HIERARCHIES OF SCHOOLS

One of the ironies of the period of Thatcher government in the 1980s was that a new Conservative Party committed to radical reform, and in particular opposed to the domination of British society by what is usually known as the Establishment, should have succeeded in education in actually strengthening the 'old guard' of private schools where the Establishment has always educated its young. The Establishment, the traditionally educated elite which had always dominated the Conservative Party as effectively as it did the Civil Service, the ancient universities, the Church of England, the Law and the armed forces, undoubtedly had its political nose put out of joint by Mrs Thatcher's brigade of radical Blue Guards. But its schools got a shot in the arm that they certainly did not expect.

Towards the beginning of Mrs Thatcher's term in office I attended a meeting of the Headmasters' Conference, the 'club' of senior private-school heads, at which the decline and possible demise of private education was being seriously discussed. Inflation and the relative success of the state sector of education were offered as the two main reasons for the headmasters' fear of extinction, and debate centred privately upon which of the less secure schools would be the first to close their doors. Less than ten years later the private schools had increased their 'market share' of pupils to more than 7 per cent of the total (see above, p. 23) and were cheerfully talking about increasing this to 10 per cent by the end of the decade.

So what had changed? Essentially two things. In the interests of a free market in education, the Thatcher government had sharply reversed the 1970s move towards uniformity in the structure of schooling. Instead of completing the system of all-embracing comprehensive schools towards which the previous Labour government and most local authorities had been moving, the Conservative government immediately repealed the obligation upon local authorities to go comprehensive, thus preserving at least some of the remaining grammar and secondary modern schools. From 1979, diversity in secondary education again became respectable within the state system, and indeed by the end of the 1980s had been greatly increased by the introduction of state-funded City Technology Colleges and grant-maintained schools which had opted out of local authority control. It looked likely to be increased further by the acceptance of new voluntary-aided schools run by religious groups such as the Muslims and by the introduction in some areas of 'magnet' schools on the American model.

It was in the interests of diversity and a free market in schooling, certainly not the Establishment, that the first Conservative administration went out of its way to boost the declining private sector – some would say, threw it a lifeline – by the introduction of the Assisted Places Scheme (APS). There is no doubt that this was the result of some skilful lobbying of the Conservative Party in opposition before the 1979 election. To understand why the Assisted Places Scheme held such importance in Conservative eyes it is necessary to go back a little further, to the early 1970s. At that period of very rapid comprehensive reorganisation it was becoming clear that a handful of semi-independent grammar schools were going to prove an anomaly in many areas. These were the 178 direct-grant schools, many of them relatively venerable foundations, most of them single-sex and a high proportion with denominational affiliations, which in 1970 accommodated 3 per cent of the secondary population and about 10 per cent of all sixth-formers. The schools were able to charge fees, but 60 per cent of their pupils and 80 per cent of their costs were funded by the state. As a group the direct-grant schools had shown no enthusiasm for integrating with comprehensive systems in their local authority areas. By 1975 the Labour government offered the direct-grant schools the choice of integration or complete independence. Almost 120 opted for independence: the rest, including most of the Roman Catholic schools, chose to remain within the state system and in many cases went comprehensive.

But those which went independent were not necessarily completely happy with their changed status. There is no doubt that the schools quite genuinely regarded the loss of their free places as a diminution of opportunity for young people from poor families. But their interest in the 'bright working-class child', tirelessly put to the Conservative opposition, was not entirely selfless. Their academic reputation had, after all, been to some extent built upon the success of young people who had come to them as state pupils, and that reputation might well suffer if the main criterion for entry to those schools became the parents' bank balance rather than the child's academic ability, as measured by tests at the age of 11.

The Assisted Places Scheme, introduced between 1979 and 1981 by the incoming Conservative government, was to some extent a straight replacement of the direct grant. It offered reduced fees to the children of parents on low incomes who passed the selection examinations of an approved number of private day schools. Parental contributions to fees were on a sliding scale ranging from full remission for parents earning less than £7,259 (in 1989). In that year the average parent paid £545 towards fees and received £2,121 in remission.

The scheme did not replace the direct grant exactly: schools with that status had been unevenly spread around the country, and the Assisted Places Scheme made some sort of geographical equality of opportunity one of its criteria, although in 1989 the DES was still trying to encourage schools to offer more places in the north-east, parts of the Midlands and South Yorkshire. More than 270 schools were participating in the scheme, offering more than 33,000 places by 1989, but Treasury restrictions on the amount of money available to fund it have meant that it has only benefited about 1 per cent of the secondary-school population, far fewer than the direct-grant schools served.

The scheme has not lived up to expectations in other ways either. Some schools have found it difficult to fill all their assisted places, especially at sixth-form level. And there has been a marked regional imbalance in take-up, with parents in the south-east of England being much more keen on obtaining assisted places for their children than in parts of the north.

Most crucially, perhaps, the APS has not in any sense provided what its founders alleged they wanted: an academic lifeline for highly academic children from deprived homes who, it was argued, would suffer academically in inner-city comprehensives. According to research which monitored the scheme from its inception, the main beneficiaries were the children of families from the middle range of occupations and social class. Only 9 per cent of APS pupils had fathers in manual occupations, and most of those were skilled workers, and although more than 30 per cent came from single-parent families, most of these were headed by mothers from middle-class backgrounds. In other words, the APS has benefited mainly the impoverished middle classes, and indeed the researchers found that some of the pupils who benefited would have attended private schools whether or not they received an assisted place. For those pupils the scheme was apparently subsidising a choice of school already determined, rather than widening parental choice, as the supporters of the scheme originally claimed.

But whatever its success, or lack of it, the Assisted Places Scheme set a tone which has persisted and intensified for a decade. By its very establishment as soon as the Conservatives were returned to power it signalled that government believed that maintained schools, particularly comprehensive schools, were inadequate to the needs of some academically inclined children, and that private secondary education was still to be regarded as the apex of a hierarchy of esteem in the minds of all right-thinking parents.

That hierarchy has been more clearly defined as the decade has gone on. By 1989 Professor Tim Brighouse of Keele University could discern a clear 'pecking order' of secondary schools for the 1990s. At the top stood the prestigious

Headmasters' Conference private schools, with the rest of the private sector not far behind. Then would come City Technology Colleges, free to pupils but far more generously funded by the state and industry and commerce than any other type of maintained school. Behind the CTCs would come the grant-maintained schools which had opted out of local authority control and would include many of the remaining grammar schools. Then the grammar schools within the LEA sector. Then rural and suburban comprehensive schools, with, at the bottom of the heap, urban comprehensive schools and the odd surviving secondary modern, bearing all the burdens of the inner cities and their inability to select children on the basis of ability, motivation or privileged catchment area.

That is a pessimistic view of the direction in which the changes of the late 1980s might lead British secondary education. How realistic is it? There is absolutely no doubt that there is a wing of the Conservative Party which resented not only the abolition of the direct grant, but the whole reorganisation of secondary education on comprehensive principles which was largely completed by the time the party regained power in 1979. If there had been a practical way of turning the clock back directly to selection they would have found it. In fact, by that stage, as Margaret Thatcher herself acknowledged tacitly when she was Secretary of State in the early 1970s, there was no practical way of reversing the comprehensive reform. Local authorities had chosen that form of organisation on demographic and economic grounds as well as on grounds of increased educational opportunity for the majority of children previously excluded from grammar schools. After the initial trauma of change they had largely won parental consent and support, with the exception perhaps of Inner London, where a large and suspicious middle class remained dissatisfied in an area of extreme urban problems. In the remaining areas with grammar schools, there were still campaigns in favour of comprehensive reform well into the 1980s. When attempts were made to turn the clock back they were vetoed by parents, as in Solihull, or the provisions on opting out in the 1988 Education Reform Act were used to protect the comprehensive nature of well-established schools, as in Milton Keynes in 1989.

But if a frontal assault on comprehensive education, with all its unwelcome egalitarian connotations, was ruled out for the Conservatives, a more subtle approach was not. Diversity within the state system accorded with the prevailing market-oriented philosophy of the government, and was not unpopular with parents, while at the same time standing a very strong chance of undermining the comprehensive philosophy which was committed to catering for the needs of all children within one school. The return of the 11-plus might be a political no-go area, but the reintroduction of selection and differentiation by means of market forces fuelled by the popular notion of parental choice was certainly a feasible means of arriving at much the same destination.

The introduction of both CTCs and grant-maintained schools lends weight to this view of what has happened to secondary education under the Conservative government. The CTCs were launched with a flourish at the 1986 Conservative Party Conference by Kenneth Baker as a means of boosting the performance of children in the inner cities who, he implied, had been so appallingly let down by the comprehensives. There were to be twenty colleges which would provide specialist teaching in science and technology and business studies for around 15,000 pupils so that those young inner-city dwellers could gain employment skills and go out and regenerate the areas in which they lived. Industry and commerce would undoubtedly assist generously in setting up these 'beacons of excellence' and parents would gain from an increase in choice of school. The plan was greeted with an ovation.

As it turned out, very little of this original prospectus stood up to the scrutiny of industry and commerce or, ultimately, to that of the Treasury. Nor did parents seem particularly impressed in many of the areas where CTCs were proposed. In the first place industry and commerce proved obstinately reluctant to come up with the substantial sums necessary to found secondary schools from scratch. By the autumn of 1989

47

three colleges were actually open – in Solihull, Nottingham and Middlesbrough. Seven or eight more should open in 1990 and the CTC Trust claims that there are another eleven in the pipeline.

Few of the CTCs so far proposed, though, are in the sort of hard-core inner-city areas that Kenneth Baker appeared to be trying to benefit by his new policy. And the major funder of the colleges has proved to be the Treasury rather than industry: by 1989 the DES admitted that it would be funding the scheme to the tune of £126.3 million over three years while industry had put up a mere £40 million so far. By the end of that year, the Treasury had effectively called a halt: the scheme was to end at twenty colleges, unless means could be found of running them with local authority support.

The major miscalculation appears to have been the cost of providing new buildings. As an alternative the Trust began to look for existing empty buildings, or even existing and functioning schools, in which to set up colleges. This brought it into immediate conflict with local authorities who were reluctant to sell, either on ideological grounds or because an existing surplus of school places would be exacerbated by the introduction of another secondary school competing for pupils. In the case of existing schools approached by the Trust, staff and parents have without exception protested strongly that they were very happy with the schools they already had. In the case of Riverside School in Bexley, south London, parental objections persuaded the local authority to drop its support for CTC status. But at Downs School in neighbouring Dartford, Kent County Council overrode parental objections, as did Croydon council over two of its schools, and the governors of the two Haberdashers' Aske's Schools in Lewisham.

Parents have much greater control over the future of their schools in the other initiative which threatens to fragment the maintained school system, the grant-maintained option. This provides for parents to vote on a proposal to take a school out of local authority control and receive its funding directly from the Department of Education and Science. This was another scheme launched by Kenneth Baker on the grounds that it would increase parental choice. Margaret Thatcher was so taken with the idea that in 1987 she expressed the hope that in the fullness of time most local authority schools would become grant-aided in this way, thus incidentally removing most of the local authorities' responsibility for providing schooling at all.

As soon as the opting-out provisions of the 1988 Act became law there was a flurry of activity, mainly amongst schools which were threatened with amalgamation or closure as part of reorganisation schemes. First to go was a grammar school in Lincolnshire which had had a row with its local authority over admissions procedures. Two comprehensives followed, both of viable size but threatened with closure or amalgamation as part of their local authorities' response to the crisis of falling rolls. When the first 63 schools to have held a ballot on opting out were analysed by the Advisory Centre for Education, it became clear that the schools most likely to be attracted by the idea of independence from local authority control were grammar schools, single-sex (particularly boys') schools and voluntary-aided schools. Leaving aside the schools simply fighting for survival by opting out, buoyed up as the process has gained momentum by the evidence that Secretaries of State will support applications from schools which would normally be regarded as far too small to be viable, it is clear that many of the rest are taking a decision which they believe will guarantee their degree of 'differentness' from the rest of the state system, which is overwhelmingly comprehensive, non-denominational and coeducational.

In a market situation, of course, it is just that degree of differentness – its unique selling point, to use the marketing jargon – which may guarantee a school's survival, particularly if it can be marketed as in some way slightly elitist. The shadow of the English public schools still falls across the whole of English education and there is no doubt that schools which cling to some of the private system's most widely marketed attributes – selective entry, formal discipline and teaching methods, large sixth forms, religious affiliation – believe that this will give them an edge in the competition for pupils, regardless of those attributes' proven educational value, or even their relevance, to the vast cross-section of children of all abilities which it is the maintained system's duty to educate.

Grant-maintained schools are not, according to the letter of the 1988 Act, an easy or an immediate route back to a selective education system. They will be funded on the same basis as the rest of the maintained system, except for the addition to their budgets of a share of those central local authority services to which they are no longer bound, a share which, it is becoming apparent, may be attractively substantial. But they must wait five years before applying to the Secretary of State for permission to change their admissions criteria. On the face of it, this leaves no immediate opportunity for existing comprehensive schools to turn themselves into grammar schools.

But the English class system works more subtly than that. Denominational schools already have a degree of control over their own admissions, and there are occasional complaints that individual Church schools use this control to exclude recruits from ethnic minority groups, although the Church of England Board of Education is committed to running its schools as a community, rather than simply an Anglican, resource. Similarly, there is little doubt that any grant-maintained comprehensive school which is oversubscribed could, if it wished, covertly discriminate against, say, children with special educational needs, or children from the more deprived parts of its catchment area, once the supervision of admission arrangements by the local authority is removed. The possibility of greater differentiation between schools is inherent to the whole concept of grant-maintained status. These schools were undoubtedly intended to be part of a hierarchy in which the ordinary neighbourhood comprehensive would be the bottom tier.

It is the avowed intention of the right-wing radicals who have advised the government on education policy to privatise education completely by providing all parents with vouchers with which they will be able to 'buy' education in either the maintained or the private sector. Greater differentiation between state schools undoubtedly takes secondary education a step down that road. So too does another major element in the 1988 Act, local management of schools (LMS).

This is a not unwelcome reform in some respects, in that it gives headteachers and governors much greater control over their own budgets, which, it is generally agreed, should make schools both more efficient and more responsive to the individual needs of their own pupils. A number of local authorities had gone some way towards delegating management and budgets to their larger schools before the Act made it compulsory for all schools with more than 200 pupils from 1989.

In terms of the Right's political agenda, though, there are two other advantages to local management on the lines laid down by the 1988 reforms. In the first place, it very usefully disaggregates the costs of individual schools, something few local authorities had ever found the time or taken the trouble to do before. Secondly, if a voucher scheme were ever to work, it would be necessary for schools to run as individual units, as they will be obliged to do to a large extent under LMS, and it would be necessary to know their precise costs – in effect, the 'fees' they would have to charge to educate a child – in order for a voucher-based market to be created.

Taken together, the introduction of diversity and competition into state education through CTCs, grant-maintained schools, and the effects of open enrolment, combined with the introduction of individual budgets controlled at school level, make the Right's educational agenda a far more feasible political proposition than it was before Mrs Thatcher came to power. We have come a long way down the road towards a system where every school is at least semi-independent and is expected to compete against every other – state or private – with the weakest, as in any market, going to the wall. We are perhaps not so far from Professor Tim Brighouse's hierarchy of schools.

But there is resistance. Local authorities, in implementing

schemes of local management for their schools, are actively seeking ways of mitigating the worst effects of the DES's regulations on schools which for historical reasons such as their small size, the age and seniority of their teaching force, their geographical position or the social deprivation of their pupils, have been 'subsidised' by the provision of extra teachers or other resources. There is certainly no acceptance in town and county halls that financially equal treatment for schools is necessarily fair treatment, and some have gone so far as to defy the letter of the local management regulations. The reaction of the DES remains to be seen.

Headteachers, too, appear to be deeply ambivalent about the inherent requirement of the new legislation that they should recruit vigorously to the extent that ultimately they close their 'rivals' down. There are powerful imperatives built into the legislation which may force them to do just that, but again the early evidence is that where they can continue to co-operate in all their interests they will seek a way to do so.

The government for its part, with the appointment of the less abrasive John MacGregor as Secretary of State, suddenly seems more sympathetic to complaints that parts of its legislation are impracticable, at least on the time scale proposed. The four-year transitional period for the introduction of LMS, for instance, looks as if it could eventually extend to ten, slowing down the elusive market system in secondary-school places to a crawl which is highly likely to be overtaken by political events.

The final imponderable, of course, is the political situation. There is no doubt that ten years of Thatcherism have moved the secondary-school system in the direction of competitiveness on the grounds that this will increase efficiency – by rationalising schools – and effectiveness – by making schools look hard at their performance. Few politicians, either at national or local level, or parents would disagree with the desirability of these two objectives, but there is sharp disagreement on the best way of achieving them. With a general election due by 1992, it seems unlikely that the 1988 Conservative reforms described earlier will have had time to justify themselves by results or become administratively irreversible before voters are required to return their verdict on more than ten years of Thatcherism. To do so, they will require the return of another Conservative administration committed to consolidating what has already been set in train.

The Labour opposition is committed to eliminating the surviving grammar schools, abolishing the Assisted Places Scheme and open enrolment, and integrating both CTCs and grant-maintained schools into the local authority structure, so eliminating at a stroke the ability of maintained schools to compete on the basis of their differentiated nature rather than the quality of their education. (This is a programme bound to meet some parental opposition if it involves closing schools.) Equally committed to raising standards and giving the maximum choice to parents, Labour rejects the market approach as damaging to the schools and children who turn out to be 'losers' and puts renewed faith instead in a planned system of comprehensive schools of equal status, working to a less rigid National Curriculum and differentially funded if necessary so as to guarantee equal opportunities to all the children within the system. Labour argues that this would be more effective than a competitive market system in eliminating the 'sink' schools all parties deplore.

A clear choice is emerging in secondary education between the market and the service ethic, perhaps the clearest ideological choice which has faced British parents since the war.

Chapter 5

THE EVOLVING SIXTH FORM

We have all wallowed in the sort of nostalgia that television packages so well. Picture the scene: green lawns and Gothic stone buildings lit by the mellow sunlight of the eternal English summer we all anticipate but seldom enjoy. Masters (very seldom mistresses), gowns billowing in the balmy breeze, chat ambiably to groups of young men (very seldom young women!) in neat blazers and ties about an abstruse point of Homer's Greek, or Renaissance poetry. A happy band of prefects keeps order amongst the boisterous but ultimately law-abiding lower school. God's in his heaven, or at least in the school chapel, and all is well with the world of the English secondary school.

It is a myth of course even in the context of the private schools, which have embraced science and technology with enthusiasm, which market themselves to 'new' parents with Madison Avenue slickness, and where Russian is more likely to be the language of choice these days than classical Greek. But it is an insidious myth, all the same, extending its hold far beyond the handful of traditional Victorian public schools which gave it birth, and nowhere influencing attitudes more potently than in discussions of the education of young people between the ages of 16 and 18.

Tradition says that such young people inhabit a 'sixth form' which in fact includes students in both their sixth and seventh years in school. This is the way it always was in the more highly academic private schools and in the grammar schools which adopted their curriculum, their mores and their values. This was therefore the way it had to be in the new comprehensive schools if they were to appear credible in public esteem as establishments able to deal successfully with the most academically inclined young people studying for A levels and wanting to go on to higher education. Hence the arguably highly damaging insistence that the early comprehensives should be far larger than most parents thought desirable in order to sustain their sixth-form numbers. Even now it is accepted that five or six forms of entry at 11 are needed to sustain a sixth form: a main school of between 750 and 900 pupils. In the early days of comprehensives, twice that number was regarded as essential.

But regardless of the best intentions of the educational planners, by the mid-1970s a vigorous free market in sixth-form students had developed. Young people themselves began to regard the age of 16 as a time for reassessment, even if they wished to continue studying full time. The boys' private schools were quick to capitalise on the terminal restlessness of fifth-formers wondering where to do their A levels. By the 1980s there was hardly a major boys' private school which did not admit girls into the sixth form, to the great chagrin of the girls'-school heads who saw some of their brightest young women being tempted away. There was movement at sixth-form level between the private and the state sectors as well. The Assisted Places Scheme, which offered help to private-school entrants at this stage, was less successful at 16 than at 11 and 13. And some state sixth-form colleges, and comprehensive and grammar-school sixth forms, soon found that they could successfully recruit disillusioned private-school pupils at 16, so usefully boosting their numbers and improving their viability.

But movement into the state sector at 16 could at best be only marginal. Keeping sixth-form numbers up to viable levels in every comprehensive school became something of a lost cause in the 1980s as the numbers of young people in secondary education began to fall dramatically. If local authorities had been able to rationalise their schools strictly in line with falling numbers, then the *status quo* – unsatisfactory enough in some areas – might have been sustained. But totally cost-effective rationalisation proved politically impossible. So, with one of the lowest staying-on rates in Europe, and declining pupil numbers, more and more local authorities began to find that the ideal of a sixth form at the summit of every comprehensive school was becoming untenable.

Worse, as schools struggled to maintain a sixth form, the extra staffing this required was increasingly being provided at the expense of younger children. Simply put, classes of 11-, 12- and 13-year-olds were becoming bigger in order to sustain classes of four, three or even two 16- and 17-year-olds who wished to study the less popular A levels. Even the educational justification for the determined struggles of schools to run small sixth forms was dubious. There was evidence from the Inspectorate that A-level pupils in very small teaching groups lacked stimulation and did rather badly in their final examinations.

Local authorities adopted two strategies to deal with the sixth-form crisis. The first, and by far the less effective, was to leave schools with their individual small sixth forms but to arrange classes co-operatively for the less popular A-level subjects. Occasionally a separate sixth-form centre would be provided for joint courses, but more usually students were expected to travel from school to school for their classes.

It was an unpopular solution to the problem with students and with parents. A-level students and teachers wasted much time travelling between different sites for different subjects, with some students taking three different subjects in three different institutions. School staff complained bitterly that they could not offer adequate supervision or pastoral care to students who were ostensibly on the sixth-form roll but who were seldom in school. The National Union of Teachers (NUT) complained that neither staying-on rates nor examination results were satisfactory in such consortium arrangements, and that students were tending to vote with their feet and find an institution which could offer all their courses under one roof. In inner London, where the ILEA proved singularly reluctant to move away from 11-to-18 all-through comprehensive schools however small their sixth forms became, parents in areas like Wandsworth, hard hit by falling rolls, actually began to demand some sort of institutional reform to solve the problem.

The second strategy was institutional reorganisation, and two versions were quickly on offer. The first, which dated back to comprehensive reorganisation itself in some areas, was to provide for all A-level students in a sixth-form college. This concentrated numbers and greatly increased the number of A-level subjects which could be offered in viable groups. The second, more radical, solution, which became increasingly popular in the 1980s, was to integrate traditional sixth-form courses into the further education college sector, so bringing all academic and vocational teaching for 16- to 19-year-olds under one roof in what became known as tertiary colleges.

The college solution to the sixth-form problem is undoubtedly popular with young people. Staying-on rates generally improve, in some cases dramatically so, when a college is opened, and when HMI surveyed ten tertiary colleges in 1989 they reported that most had established good links with local secondary schools, meeting one of the main worries amongst parents when a college solution is proposed. They also commented favourably on teaching standards, A-level results, and on the standards of pastoral care and guidance available to students, another anxiety for parents when contemplating the pros and cons of the traditionally small, close-knit sixth form as against a generally much larger college.

But the organisation of post-16 education cannot be considered as simply a logistical problem. If there is an educational crisis in Britain, and with South Korea now surging well ahead of the UK in the numbers of young people it chooses to educate beyond the age of 16, it is certainly arguable that such a crisis not only exists but is worsening, it is at its most acute beyond the minimum school-leaving age. As governments of all political complexions have been saying since the mid-1970s, even if standards have been rising, they have not been rising fast enough for us to equip our workforce with the level of general education or vocational skills they will need for the changing circumstances of the 1990s. And that leaves on one side the liberal argument that a democratic society benefits in far more than economic ways for having a well-educated population.

Incredibly there are signs that even in the area where Britain has traditionally been most successful – educating the minority of young people who study for academic qualifications at 18 and go on into higher education – something is going badly wrong. When the A-level results came out in the summer of 1988, it became clear that although A-level numbers overall had begun to increase again after reaching a plateau, there was a continuing decline in the number of young people taking the exam in sciences, modern languages and even mathematics. The following year, with overall numbers up, there had been a slight improvement in modern language entries, largely, it appeared, as a result of more attractive syllabuses, but the trend in science remained downwards.

As the secretary of one examination board commented, that sets up a vicious spiral – fewer students taking A levels means fewer going into higher education courses in related areas, and ultimately fewer going back into the schools to teach. By the following year, it was clear that the shortage of teachers in those three areas, and in some others, was reaching crisis proportions.

Politically, few people disagree that something radical needs to be done to keep more young people in Britain in education until they are 18 and beyond. The government has now set as its target the doubling of higher education student numbers within 25 years. The success of this policy must to a large extent be dependent on the success of education between the ages of 16 and 18, where expectations for most young people remain traditionally far too low. More than 50 per cent of young people are still lost to education completely at this point. Only 17 per cent take academic A-level examinations. For our nearest neighbour, France, the objective for the 1990s is to raise the number of students taking the *baccalauréat*, the equivalent of three A levels as an entry qualification for higher education, to 70 per cent of the age-group. We are, in international terms, hardly at the starting gate

in terms of raising the educational performance of our 17-
and 18-year-olds.

But although the objective is agreed, there is certainly no
consensus on how to attract more 16-year-olds to stay in
education beyond the minimum school-leaving age and to
ensure that amongst those who do stay on sufficient numbers
are equipped with the high-level skills in science, maths and
technology that a post-industrial economy needs and, arguably, any well-educated person ought to have.

The Conservative government has balked at the full-scale
reform of A levels proposed by the Higginson Committee in
1988 (*Report of the Higginson Committee on A Levels*; HMSO).
The conclusion of that inquiry, the latest of a series spanning
fifteen years and getting nowhere, was that the present three-
subject A-level course should be replaced by five 'leaner' subjects, which would either allow, or could be used to insist,
that all students followed a broad course including maths and
science to 18. The report was almost unanimously welcomed
by educationists and by industry and commerce, but was
rejected by the Prime Minister, Margaret Thatcher, on the
grounds that traditional A levels were an academic bastion
which could not be breached.

Even so, it is clear that the academic A-level route is evolv-
ing and will continue to evolve. To some extent, politicians
have themselves opened up a route towards a broader sixth-
form education through the introduction of AS (advanced sup-
plementary) examinations. These are worth 'half' an A level
and at least in theory could be used to increase the number
of subjects studied to four, five or even six. In theory they
could also be used to improve the 'spread' of subjects taken
across the humanities/science/social science divisions, but so
far there is little evidence that students are rushing to take
'complementary' subjects – maths or science with arts A
levels, or a language with the sciences, for instance. Some
schools seem content to use AS levels as little more than a
staging post on the way to A level which, as Angela Rumbold,
the Minister of State for Education, pointed out somewhat
sharply in 1989, was not quite what the government

intended. Even so, the AS level is the best hope of increasing both subject numbers and breadth that is likely to emerge before the general election of 1991 or 1992.

The success of AS levels will depend in the short term on the attitude of higher education admissions tutors to them. University vice-chancellors and polytechnic directors have collectively welcomed the 'half' A levels, but unless these quickly become established as sound currency for entry to specific courses, and particularly to oversubscribed courses like medicine and law, then schools will be reluctant to advise students to take them in preference to the traditional three A levels.

But there are less overt changes afoot too. Both the GCSE and the National Curriculum which is to be introduced over the next five or six years emphasise practical and skill-based aspects of learning as well as knowledge and understanding. It was always clear that the more traditional, knowledge-based syllabuses of many A-level examinations would prove daunting to some pupils who transferred to them from GCSE. Some schools report the need for special courses to prepare students for A level after GCSE. But the problem is more complex than this. Students who come to sixth forms after a diet of problem-solving and project-based work can find the more traditional note-taking approach thoroughly demotivating. Ironically it is no longer even a good preparation for higher education, as many university and polytechnic courses have themselves moved towards more modern and experiential teaching and learning methods.

Given this two-way squeeze, it is hardly surprising that the examination boards, under pressure from the schools, have begun to modernise their A-level syllabuses. Content is being reduced, problem-solving, project work, and assessed course-work are being increased, less emphasis is being placed on an all-or-nothing final examination which an astonishing 30 per cent of candidates fail. And given the apparent success of GCSE methods in motivating pupils at 16, in raising standards of performance, as far as can be judged from the first two years' results, and in improving the staying-on rate, it would be surprising if a move in the same direction at 18 did not in the long run have the same sort of effect.

But even if A-level entries doubled, these would still be taken only by a third of young people. After 16, the majority of young people who currently stay in education at all, do so either to repeat GCSEs or to take a wide range of vocational and semi-vocational courses either at school or in further education colleges. The government has made a start at rationalising what was a confusing jungle of post-16 qualifications in vocational subjects, but many of their critics argue that they have not yet gone far enough in other ways. The Confederation of British Industry has called for a significantly increased staying-on rate at 16, a financial safety net to ensure that no student is deterred from staying on by lack of means, further reform of vocational qualifications and, most radically, and surprisingly from an employers' organisation, a breakdown of the present sharp division between academic and vocational education. BP, the petroleum giant, in a report commissioned originally for its own purposes but eventually published, complained in 1989 that 16-to-18 education was 'elitist and confusing'. They called for radical reform to bridge the academic–vocational divide, with the National Curriculum extended to 18, financial incentives for 16-year-olds to stay on, if necessary by extending the higher education loans scheme due to be introduced in 1990, and less specialised first degrees. The Labour Party is not unsympathetic to these objectives, and welcomed the demise of the Youth Training Scheme, which it says has not delivered high-quality education and training for its participants. Labour also wants a clear route into higher education for those young people who opt to take vocational rather than academic courses at 16.

Whatever the political situation over the next few years, it seems inevitable that some of these changes will come about. The imperatives are economic and increasingly urgent if this country is not to be left behind in the international race to build up a highly qualified and flexible workforce for the 1990s and beyond. But there are obstacles, quite apart from the nature of the courses on offer. One is finance. It is now clear that modern courses and teaching methods can motivate young people in a way previously dismissed as impossible, and some of those more highly motivated young people are responding by choosing to stay at school or college beyond the age of 16. Others, though, particularly from poorer families, still find the temptation of a wage packet at 16, however dead-end the job it is attached to, irresistible. Shirley Williams, as Secretary of State for Education, attempted to introduce grants for post-16 students before the Labour government fell in 1979. The idea has not been revived by the Conservative government, although it has proposed training vouchers for school-leavers, but it is still supported by the Labour Party. Some sort of assistance for poorer students is probably essential if full-time participation targets are to be significantly improved.

Another obstacle is, inevitably, the current state of institutional arrangements for students over 16. Tiny sixth forms are not cost-effective, educationally effective or attractive to potential students. Colleges for the over-16s are all of those things. But in order to switch from one to the other, some larger sixth forms, as well as very small ones, generally have to be subsumed into colleges as well. This can be expensive in terms of start-up costs and is very often fiercely resisted by parents and teachers who are still under the influence of that potent myth – the exclusive, academically high-powered quasi-public-school sixth. And since the passage of the 1988 Education Reform Act, schools determined to retain their sixth forms at all costs have had an extra weapon in their armoury, the ability to opt out of local authority control, which in some areas has virtually put all attempts to concentrate post-16 provision into cold storage.

If Britain is serious about boosting the educational achievement of its young people, change has to come to the traditional sixth form. It is simply too narrow and too exclusive in its academic focus to do the job that has to be done. But at the end of the 1980s, it is not at all clear how institutional reform for the over-16s can quickly be brought about, how in fact a mass education system can escape from the long shadow of the Victorian public schools.

Chapter 6

THE CHANGING CURRICULUM

The curriculum of British secondary schools has traditionally been the private preserve of headteachers and their staff. Boards of governors might technically have had oversight of what was taught in their school, but few governors in the 1960s or early 1970s had the temerity to raise curriculum issues at all. If, as was often jokingly suggested, a headteacher felt like offering nothing but maths and Marxism to pupils, there was nothing much anyone could do to stop it.

In practice, of course, it was not quite like that. The secondary curriculum was an extremely traditional plant, well rooted, like the sixth form, in the public schools of the nineteenth century. Long after the Second World War maintained grammar schools were still dividing their pupils into classical (the most prestigious), modern language and scientific streams at the age of 13 or 14 and not only allowing but positively encouraging young people to drop science and in some cases even mathematics long before they had gained an O-level qualification in them. The secondary modern schools, and the new comprehensives, very conscious of their lack of status in the educational scheme of things, often fell into the same trap, offering little more at first than a watered-down grammar-school curriculum, which was itself a watered-down public-school curriculum. Right across secondary education, what was taught was highly literary – it was quite possible to get to university having spent the last two years at school studying Greek poets, Latin poets and historians and either ancient history or English or French poets and dramatists, and be regarded as a great academic success. Science, which was taught to a very high standard to those who opted for it in the sixth form, remained largely theoretical with practical applications and skills counting for little. Few other industrialised countries allowed such rigid specialisation so early.

This could not go on, and the pressures for change, when they came in the 1960s, were from two directions. The first was the increasing consensus that Britain risked lagging behind other countries in the technological and scientific race for success. This was the time of Prime Minister Harold Wilson's ambition to forge a new Britain in the 'white heat of technology', and a secondary-school system which allowed many of its brightest young people to drop out of science and technology at 14 was clearly not going to take the nation very far in that direction.

The second pressure came from the realisation that a high proportion of young people in secondary education were becoming demotivated and bored by the watered-down version of the academic curriculum they were being offered, and were therefore actively disruptive in schools long before they reached the newly raised school-leaving age of 16. If schools were at last to fulfil the promise of the 1944 Education Act and provide a genuine secondary education for all young people up to the age of 16, it was likely that they would have to provide a rather different menu from the one on offer in the grammar schools. So the move towards a more relevant, and possibly even more vocational curriculum, at that stage merely for the less motivated pupils in secondary education, was born.

Curriculum research and development in secondary education began in earnest in the 1960s, much of it stimulated and funded by the Schools Council, a body which brought together representatives of the teaching profession, industry and government. They were not alone: the Nuffield Foundation funded work on science and language teaching, and the Schools Mathematics Project, which introduced new content and teaching methods, had its roots in the private-school system. There was a burgeoning of experiment and innovation in schools which spanned the whole curriculum and which began to influence the traditional examination system as the new Certificate of Secondary Education promoted new methods of examination and assessment for the 80 per cent or so of pupils who were not thought to be capable of O levels.

Curriculum reformers were not without their critics, who saw in some of the changes a lowering of standards and the provision of easy options. In any case, progress was piecemeal and relatively slow. Control of what any individual school taught still lay with the head. For every school which was insisting by the late 1970s that all students study science and technology to 16, there were probably a dozen which were not, as HMI reported. For every school which had adopted some of the more pupil-friendly schemes of work for slower learners, there were others still clinging to traditional, and often demotivating, syllabuses. Given an economic recession following the oil crisis of 1973, and the fact, increasingly obvious to politicians if not to all educationists, that many of Britain's industrial competitors were racing ahead as they pushed up staying-on rates at 16 and 18 and raised levels of attainment, it was not surprising that by 1976 Prime Minister James Callaghan should be announcing the end of the headteachers' monopoly on the nature and pace of curriculum reform.

Her Majesty's Inspectorate and the civil servants at the DES spearheaded the assault on the 'secret garden' of the curriculum. In a series of reports both groups outlined where they thought the various subjects of the traditional secondary-school curriculum should be going and what sort of balance should be kept between the different elements at least up to the age of 16. Whether in terms of subjects, or in terms of what HMI defined as 'areas of experience' – the scientific, the linguistic, the mathematical, the technical and so on – it was clear that the general thrust was towards a broader, less specialised education for all children up to the age of 16 including a common 'core' of, at the very least, maths, English and science. The writing was on the wall for the peculiarly British habit of allowing so many young people, particularly girls, to drop out of science and technology at 14.

At the same time there was also growing pressure for a change in teaching methods in secondary education. The

Inspectorate, industry, the Royal Society of Arts, and curriculum reformers in the schools and colleges, began to demand a more practically oriented approach to secondary education for all young people, not just for slower learners. They were proposing something more in line with the progressive methods of the good British primary school which successfully motivates children by encouraging learning through discovery, problem-solving and projects of varying degrees of complexity. As the Royal Society of Arts complained when it launched its 'Education for Capability' scheme for schools, British education had traditionally emphasised knowledge and understanding at the expense of skills and problem-solving, knowing and criticising at the expense of making and doing. It was time for a change.

The incoming Conservative government in 1979 was, like its successors, no respecter of professional sensitivities. During his time as Secretary of State for Education, Sir Keith Joseph launched two initiatives which were to take on board much of the criticism of secondary education of the previous decade. On behalf of his own ministry, he finally endorsed the amalgamation of GCE O-level examinations with the Certificate of Secondary Education, which had been under discussion for almost a decade. This not only ended a dual system of examinations which caused the schools much practical difficulty and employers great confusion, but also gave official blessing to an exam system which, while far more centralised than ever before, was also far more radical in both syllabus content and methods of teaching and assessment. The new GCSE has at a stroke introduced modern teaching methods to all secondary schools for 14- to 16-year-olds. It was a bold and imaginative decision for a Conservative minister to take, and is still much criticised on the far Right for allegedly 'lowering standards'. But it is evidently being justified by results: levels of attainment have risen in the first two years of the new examination, teachers report that motivation is improved, and the staying-on rate at 16 has begun to rise again after falling back in the early 1980s.

Sir Keith Joseph also endorsed an even more radical

initiative from the Manpower Services Commission (MSC), which in 1982 launched the Technical and Vocational Education Initiative (TVEI: see below, p. 69). The sensitivities trampled upon by David Young (now Lord Young; then Secretary of State for Employment and a moving force behind TVEI) in this case were those of the local education authorities, who found themselves for the first time being offered money by a government department which had little connection with education for a centrally directed scheme with some very serious strings attached. Having got over their chagrin at this constitutionally highly unusual intervention from a non-education Ministry, the LEAs generally found that they could, in fact, meet the MSC's breakneck timetable for setting up pilot schemes in some of their schools. The money, after all, was generous, amounting initially to about £600,000 per group of schools and colleges involved. The reaction from the schools was generally that they did not much care where the money came from: TVEI funding allowed time to invest in and develop areas of the curriculum and teaching strategies which they would have liked to explore much earlier if funding had been available.

The GCSE was introduced under the most appallingly difficult circumstances for the schools, with the first courses scheduled to start in the autumn of 1986 for examination in 1988. The go-ahead was given at the height of the teachers' industrial action over pay and the time allowed for training and preparation was generally agreed to be a year too short, although pleas for an extension fell on deaf ears at the DES. Schools regularly reported that training was chaotic and inadequate, reorganisation of the examining boards which the new qualification entailed was causing administrative difficulties, textbooks and materials were not adequately funded and that marking and assessment schemes and procedures were not ready until long after the children had begun their two-year courses.

In the circumstances, the first two years of GCSE have been a triumph, and one which could only have been brought about by the total determination of the teaching profession to make a reform in which most of them believed succeed. In their report on the first two years of the examination, HMI concluded that it had led to significant improvements in standards in the fourth and fifth years of secondary education. There had been, they found, a marked improvement in both oral and written work, more and better practical and investigative work and that pupils had shown what they knew, understood and could do, especially in their coursework.

Inevitably there were hiccups, which both HMI and the Schools Examinations and Assessment Council identified. Some teachers and pupils were overburdened by the coursework element of some subjects, marking and moderation procedures proved difficult for teachers new to them (mainly those who had not had experience of CSE), computer and administrative failures meant that some of the first results in 1988 were agonisingly late. Some schools complained that the most able pupils were not stretched by the new exam while, conversely, others found it daunting for their less able young people. But none of these problems is insoluble in the long run, nor did they detract from the official verdict that GCSE had proved its worth very quickly – not least by apparently boosting the staying-on rate in its very first year.

TVEI turned out to be a rather more problematic innovation. The initial aim of the project was to devise courses for young people between the ages of 14 and 18, initially in schools but possibly for the older age groups in colleges of further education, which would have a more technical and vocational bias than the normal academic curriculum. It was not to be a project specifically for less academically able children, and certainly the pilot schemes attempted to recruit young people of all abilities and both sexes, although it soon became apparent that it was not easy to persuade girls of 14 to choose technical courses, however well funded and well promoted. Nor was TVEI intended to be mere job training, although in the event it tended to prove most attractive in many schools to young people who wanted to leave at 16 and go straight into work.

There was no doubt that schools, initially given quite large sums of money, welcomed the opportunity TVEI gave them to experiment. No two pilot TVEI schemes were the same, although all had to meet certain basic criteria to satisfy the MSC: work experience and careers counselling, profile reports on students rather than traditional school reports, residential experience, attention to equal opportunities and a work-related bias to aspects of the curriculum including science and technology, business studies, information technology, maths and English. Many of the schools and colleges involved in the pilot schemes spent a great deal of their MSC allowance on information technology hardware and software, an investment that many admitted benefited the whole school as well as the selected TVEI pupils. Some local authorities set up TVEI centres, open to pupils from several schools, where capital equipment could be most cost-effective.

TVEI has not been without its critics, particularly those bemused by the pervasive and often quite incomprehensible jargon which has grown up around the scheme. Others have resented the fact that in some schools it has tended to become the preserve of the less academically able, instead of a course appropriate to the whole ability range, as was originally intended, and that for some children it verges on job training at an absurdly early age, however pre-vocational rather than vocational it is supposed to be. The NUT has warned that the funds available to extend the scheme to all schools − £90 million for more than 4,000 secondary schools whereas the first 62 projects ran on just under £30 million − will simply not be sufficient.

Yet in spite of these reservations, and the research finding that so far TVEI has done little to improve examination performance amongst young people participating, there are still many teachers and parents who have welcomed the innovation as a genuine contribution to motivating young people who might otherwise have either dropped out of education or become bored and possibly disruptive during their last two years at school. And there is no doubt that in some schools TVEI has, as the MSC intended, begun to influence the nature of the education offered to the whole age-group.

With the introduction of the National Curriculum in the 1990s for the 14-to-16 age-group, however, the future of TVEI looks, to say the least, problematic. Much is made of the possibility of integration with the National Curriculum requirements, an ideal to which both education ministers and the Training Agency (which has succeeded the MSC) subscribe publicly. And for young people post-16 there is now some experience of fulfilling TVEI aims alongside other courses such as A level. But many headteachers, already despairing of fitting the ten (eleven in Wales) National Curriculum subjects into GCSE timetables, can see little chance of preserving even a vestige of TVEI-style courses after 1994.

This is not to say that TVEI will not linger on: profiling, introduced into many schools as part of TVEI, has been taken up with enthusiasm, although hopes of a national record of achievement scheme have been dashed. Work experience has become an integral part of the programme of many schools for fifth- and sixth-formers. Links between schools and industry have been strengthened enormously over the last ten years as a result of both TVEI and other schemes, such as the London Compact, work shadowing in industry and commerce by teachers, and the greater involvement of local industry and commerce in school government. None of this will necessarily trickle into the sand. But many questions remain to be answered about the exact place of such initiatives in the new world of the National Curriculum and its all-embracing assessment system which, as has been said many times since it was launched for consultation in 1987, bears a distinct resemblance to the state school curriculum enshrined in law in 1902.

Chapter 7

THE NATIONAL CURRICULUM

Under the terms of the 1988 Education Act, the school curriculum in England and Wales was effectively nationalised. What pupils in maintained schools are to be taught between the ages of 5 and 16 in ten (in Wales eleven) major areas of the curriculum will in future be laid down by regulation by the Secretary of State. He or she will be advised on curriculum matters by two committees, the National Curriculum Council, and the Schools Examinations and Assessment Council (appointed by the Secretary of State), but the ultimate decision will be the minister's alone.

This total reversal in the way English education is controlled, effectively removing power over the curriculum from teachers, governors and local authorities and placing it in the hands of politicians at national level, took a little over ten years to accomplish, from the time James Callaghan ruffled educational feathers by criticising the 'secret garden' to the publication in 1987 of Kenneth Baker's proposals on curriculum and assessment preparatory to the 1988 Act. It is worth taking a little time to consider just how this political revolution came about, before considering whether its effect on secondary education will, in the long run, be benign or malign, or even feasible.

There is no doubt that some of the public disillusion which swept the Conservatives to power in 1979 was focused on education. The Labour government had become critical of the performance of the schools, and there was a growing feeling amongst all sectors of society that the professionals could and should be more accountable to their clients. In education the focus was particularly on what were perceived to be unsatisfactory standards, on new rights for parents, who were beginning to seek – and in some areas gain – more involvement in school government, more choice in secondary-school places and more responsive complaints procedures when things went wrong. If there was opposition to the spirit of the Taylor Report, for instance, which proposed greater involvement for parents as school governors, it was largely bureaucratic rather than ideological, and local authorities of all political persuasions were beginning to move in Taylor's direction before the Conservatives legislated on school government for the first time in 1981, and again in 1986.

Progress was being made on accountability, though it was slow. So too was progress on curriculum reform, which by the early 1980s had reached the point at which there was some consensus about the direction in which secondary schools ought to go, but no direct means of forcing them to get there. The consensus was perhaps best expressed in Sir Keith Joseph's White Paper, *Better Schools*, published in 1985. By the next election, Sir Keith hoped, AS-level and GCSE courses would be well under way, records of achievement would be widespread, initial teacher training would have been reformed according to national criteria, a scheme for regular teacher appraisal would have been launched, new-style governing bodies would be in place, TVEI would be widely established, and broad agreement would have been reached on national objectives for the 5-to-16 curriculum.

It is at least arguable that those aims would have been achieved by the end of the decade, had nothing else been proposed by Sir Keith's successor. It tackled, in a way which teachers on the whole accepted, most of the deficiencies which had been identified in the system – less than rigorous teacher training, lack of appraisal of teacher performance, the need for greater accountability to parents and the community through reformed governing bodies. It offered the opportunity for two major new curriculum and assessment initiatives, GCSE and TVEI, to find their way and produce results, backed up by records of achievement, which were also widely welcomed by schools, parents and employers. And broad agreement on curriculum objectives, certainly at secondary level, was not so far away. Sir Keith's own definition of a curriculum which should be broad, balanced, relevant and differentiated, had few serious critics, although there was some veiled worry about differentiation, but professional opinion seemed to be hardening around the introduction of a compulsory 'core curriculum' up to the age of 16 which would include for all children compulsory English, maths and science, plus optional courses across the humanities, languages, technical, practical and creative subjects. The consensus also gaining ground, with the strong support of the Association for Science Education, the science teachers' organisation which was heavily involved in curriculum development, was that compulsory science to 16 should also be broad and balanced so as to prevent young people, especially girls, opting out of the physical sciences at 14. A great deal of work was being done by the Secondary Science Curriculum Review and others to provide suitable courses to co-ordinate chemistry, physics and biology within about 20 per cent of the timetable for older secondary students.

A period of a few years for innovation to be followed by evaluation might have seemed appropriate, but politics dictated otherwise. In 1985 Sir Keith Joseph was replaced by Kenneth Baker, whose immediate political brief was to settle the long and damaging teachers' pay dispute. But by 1987 he was as willing as Mrs Thatcher herself, under pressure from the Right which was clamouring for a 'return to basics' in the classroom and the introduction of market forces in the school system, to put education at the top of the political agenda in time for the general election.

The Conservatives went to the country that year committed to a radical reform programme which included, amongst much more, a national curriculum and regular assessment of children at the ages of 7, 11, 14 and 16. Within months of their re-election, the plans had been fleshed out in a series of hurriedly issued consultation documents, most of which appeared during the school holidays. Even so they produced an unprecedented barrage of responses from local authorities, academics, teachers and headteachers, unions and parents, almost all of which advised that while the objectives of the reforms might be acceptable the means of achieving them were variously overprescriptive, overcomplicated, expensive, bureaucratic and, in the concentration of power they placed in the hands of the Secretary of State, potentially undemocratic. Mr Baker refused to publish the responses, which eventually appeared in Julian Haviland's book, *'Take Care, Mr Baker!'*. Nevertheless the proposals passed through Parliament, virtually unchanged, to become law in 1988.

The National Curriculum lays down that secondary-school pupils must study three core subjects – maths, English and science – and a further seven foundation subjects – technology, history, geography, art, music, physical education and a modern foreign language – until the age of 16. Pupils in Wales must also study Welsh, and religious education (RE) remains compulsory in all state schools unless parents ask for their children to be exempted. Pupils will be assessed in all these subjects (except RE) at 14 and at 16, where the National Curriculum assessment will eventually be integrated with GCSE.

Detailed programmes of study and attainment targets are being laid down by parliamentary regulation, and by 1989 working parties had considered the maths and science requirements, and primary-school English, and regulations were implemented. Secondary-school English is to follow close behind; the deliberations of the working parties on technology and history teaching are well under way; geography and modern languages have begun work. Eleven-year-olds began work on National Curriculum maths and science in autumn 1989; English and technology should follow in 1990, history and geography the year after and art, music, PE and possibly modern languages in 1992.

Assessment will be introduced more slowly as pupils who have started National Curriculum syllabuses at 11 and 14 reach the ages of 14 and 16. So 14-year-olds will be assessed in maths and science for the first time in 1993, and in English in 1994, with the whole process not expected to be running until 1996 and 1997. This assumes that all the development work currently being undertaken on assessment goes smoothly, and both the finance and the political will are found to complete what will be a far more elaborate structure of external testing than is employed by any other developed country.

There is still considerable hostility to the National Curriculum and to the proposed testing system on the grounds of both undesirability and impracticability. To take the latter and more widely argued point first, it is generally conceded by secondary heads that curriculum and examination development in the 1960s and 1970s had been extremely fruitful in helping to develop more relevant and motivating courses for young people, but that it had resulted in a certain level of chaos. Families moving from one area of the country to another could not be at all sure that their children would be able to follow the same syllabuses or subjects or take the same examinations in their new school. When, for instance, the new Schools Examinations and Assessment Council analysed the examination courses being offered in secondary schools in 1988 they came up with an alarming total of 900 GCSE and 850 non-GCSE qualifications.

A thousand flowers had bloomed and the jungle had become, to put it mildly, a little overgrown. There was not much objection to the sort of rationalisation of courses which had in any case been set in train by the establishment of national criteria for GCSE, which itself had the potential for standardising to some extent what most young people would learn in their last two years at school.

Nor was there serious opposition by the mid-1980s to the notion of a core curriculum to put an end to early specialisation which cut off many young people, especially girls and the less able, from whole areas of employment and further study at the early age of 14. But it was obvious from the very first published version of the National Curriculum in the summer of 1987 that what was proposed went very much further than the consensus. It imposed ten (in Wales eleven) compulsory subjects to the age of 16, when the normal GCSE load for most children was seven or eight. It threatened to eliminate some subjects such as business studies, home economics, drama, classics, a second modern language and even the Conservatives' own TVEI, from the timetable entirely.

Indeed it soon became clear that even fitting in the ten or eleven compulsory elements was going to be difficult when the DES conceded that what it was proposing amounted not to 100 per cent but much more like 120 per cent of a timetable for 14- to 16-year-olds. As the various working parties reported, each claiming their own share of school time, the sums became increasingly bizarre and the chances of retaining any subject options at all for 14-year-olds began to look increasingly remote. The National Curriculum plus a little time for personal and social education looks like being the whole curriculum for most secondary children in future; but that depends on whether schools can adapt to what is now required, whether teachers surplus to requirements in business studies and home economics, for instance, can be shed, and enough staff found to expand the areas of study now in favour, such as science and technology. All this, at a time of general teacher shortage and a degree of demoralisation in the schools, looks problematic, to say the least.

The National Curriculum also introduces another level of external assessment at 14, across ten or eleven subjects, with apparently massive teacher involvement in marking and moderation, just two years before GCSE, which itself had placed additional burdens of that sort on the teaching force. There is also a major problem to be resolved by the time of the first 16-year-old assessments in 1994, which is how the new ten-level system is to fit with GCSE grades A to G, or indeed whether a dual system of assessment at the minimum school-leaving age is either desirable or feasible. There is no doubt that many secondary schools would be furious to see all the work that has gone into the development of GCSE being undermined in any way by the new system. Government statements so far have floated the possibilities of splitting the A grade at GCSE, currently attained by about 10 per cent of candidates, into two, providing 'half GCSEs' in some subjects, and of providing 'fast streams' to allow 'bright' children to take extra subject options. On the other hand,

John MacGregor, Kenneth Baker's successor, has refused to accept that GCSE should provide a certificate for young people achieving the lowest grades. There are a host of practical issues to resolve in this area before 1994, some of them with very serious implications for the certification of school-leavers.

Surveys show that most teachers sympathise with the general thrust of the National Curriculum. There is a general welcome for the programmes of study in maths and science for secondary pupils which have been published so far, and an acceptance that these will make progression much easier for schools to monitor and parents to understand, as children work their way through the system. It will also be very much easier in future for pupils to change schools during their secondary school careers without losing out academically.

But few secondary heads believe that in secondary schools either the ten-subject curriculum, especially beyond the age of 14, or the amount of assessment proposed, is practicable. Most are convinced that the extra staff and resources necessary to implement such a radical scheme will not be forthcoming: and the more serious the country's economic difficulties become, the less they are inclined to believe that the Treasury will look kindly on requests for the sort of funding they think the legislation requires for effective implementation. Most view the prospect of implementing the National Curriculum and assessment with considerable trepidation, especially at a time when other extra burdens are being placed on schools as a result of the same legislation – in particular the new responsibility for financial management, which will be phased in by 1993. The extremely competent and devoted secondary head who confessed that he attended meetings with other heads in late 1989 in moods which swung from hysteria to anger is by no means unusual.

There is also continuing concern about the dangers of political intervention in the curriculum inherent in the Act, and it is here that worry about the basic undesirability of some aspects of the National Curriculum focuses. All the subjects which have reached the regulatory stage so far have shown both ministers and MPs ready to weigh into academic areas where they would not have dreamed of intervening even five years ago. The signs are that these arguments will become ever more fierce as the government-appointed working parties and ministers get to grips with syllabuses where judgements are inevitably more subjective and therefore very much more contentious. The first three working parties, on science, maths and English, all produced reports which were more concerned with how, rather than what, children are taught and learn. The English working party, for instance, refused to produce a list of 'approved' authors for English literature, and resisted attempts by the politicians to be extremely prescriptive about when and how English grammar should be introduced. All the groups shied away from narrow rote learning – the return to the sort of 'basics' which some politicians and others demanded – and tried to devise ways to assess children's skills and understanding as well as knowledge. Most of what the working parties recommended and ministers accepted fell into the mainstream of current teaching practice and curriculum reform, the same mainstream which had underpinned GCSE, although Mr Baker felt no scruples at intervening in relatively minor ways – over the use of calculators in maths, over grammar teaching and poetry in English, and on the amount of time children must spend on science in the later stages of secondary education. The National Curriculum Council, which also offers its advice to the Secretary of State, wanted to insist that all 14- to 16-year-olds spend 20 per cent of their time on science. Mr Baker allowed the possibility of a 12.5 per cent option, a decision which some critics argue will allow girls and the less able still to opt out of a full science curriculum.

And there are undoubtedly fierce arguments to come. Both history and geography and the arts are areas of the curriculum at secondary level where different philosophies of education may collide head on. Reactions by teachers to the interim report of the geography working party reveal fierce resistance to the threat of a return to a traditionalist, fact-dominated approach to the subject. There are those who argue that such professional disagreements should be resolved by professionals not politicians.

But so far, the politicians have shown no reticence in intervening, even in the most contentious areas of the curriculum. John MacGregor has already indicated to the history working party that he would like greater emphasis on chronology and on British history. The history working party's interim report has revealed the dangers of too specific a list of topics in subjects where schoolchildren cannot possibly learn everything, and some selection has to be made. The Historical Association, which consulted widely with practising teachers on the interim report, found a general acceptance of the principles upon which it was drawn up, but severe misgivings amongst some teachers about the omission of crucial aspects of history such as the Reformation, the First and Second World Wars, the rise of Fascism and Nazism, and the history of Ireland, all of them arguably essential topics if schoolleavers are to gain any grasp of why Britain, Europe and the world are as they are now. The second report aroused equal outrage over its proposals on the treatment of the British Empire.

But there is a more fundamental question, and that is whether politicians, of any persuasion, should have this level of detailed control over what is taught in schools. We now have a system of curriculum control under which any incoming minister may quite legally adapt what is taught in schools to suit his or her own predilections: the history of Northern Ireland, or the economics of the Third World, may be in today and out tomorrow; information about birth control may form part of the biology curriculum now, but not if a Roman Catholic takes over the Department of Education. The possibilities are endless, some quite innocuous, others potentially totalitarian. In what has by any standards been a massive shift of power over what children are taught from the schools to central government, it may be that the 1988 legislation has gone at least one step too far, especially at a time when classes are more ethnically, culturally and religiously mixed than ever before.

Chapter 8
BETTER SCHOOLS?

There can be no one connected with education, from the Secretary of State to the humblest 'helper', who would not like to see standards rise. There can be few parents who would not like their children to 'do better', whether they are ambitious professionals convinced their children are 'not being stretched' and weighing up the advantages and disadvantages of state versus private education, or the anxious family of a special needs child hoping against hope that basic literacy may be achieved. It is small wonder that when a panacea is offered — whether in the form of a National Curriculum, regular spelling tests, or a dose of old-time religion — somebody somewhere, parent or professional, falls for it.

The reality, of course, is more complex and infinitely more time-consuming. All the evidence is that judging by the relatively simple measures we have available, standards in secondary education have been rising steadily, though relatively slowly, since the Second World War. More young people are gaining examination qualifications, more are staying in education at 16, more are going on to higher education. But although it is possible to measure trends of this sort, this does not necessarily tell us what we are doing right to bring about this modest improvement, or indeed what we must do better if we seriously wish to accelerate away much faster in secondary education, as all the politicians say we must if we are to remain competitive in international terms. It does not explain, for instance, why the increase in young people going into higher education is largely confined to the children of the professional and managerial middle classes. Or why some children in adolescence appear to be turned off school completely, to the despair of parents and teachers. Or why, as research tells us, some schools are considerably more effective than others in all sorts of ways.

What parents choosing a secondary school would like is a simple indicator of quality. What they generally get are school examination results, and if and when the National Curriculum is fully operative, they will have yet another set of statistics, the results of the 14-year-old assessments, to pore over. In other words, we will be even more persistent than we are now about measuring children regularly (and it is as well to remember that some countries such as the USA do not have any public examination system at all, or rely, like the Netherlands, on a single test at school-leaving age) without being any more sure than we were before about what is likely to make them grow intellectually so as to perform better in the tests.

As far as the government was concerned, of course, testing was to engage the issue of standards from an entirely different angle. One of the quite overt objectives of the proposed regular system of assessment, and the publication of results, was to enable parents to make comparisons between schools in a more market-oriented system which should, it was argued, of itself raise standards by forcing poor schools out of business.

There is a snag to this simplistic view of the efficacy of tests. As the Task Group on Assessment and Testing (TGAT) which advised the government on the new assessment system pointed out, published test results must be treated with some caution if they are to be used to compare schools. Common sense tells us that some schools start with an inbuilt advantage when it comes to getting children through examinations: their pupils come from supportive homes where English is the first language, books and other cultural activities are readily made available, there is a tradition of staying on at school and going on to higher education, there is enough money to keep children well clothed, well fed, and enough time and energy to keep them emotionally secure and protected from the worst dangers of modern life. Schools with large numbers of such privileged children amongst their intake will tend to produce good examination results, while those with fewer will generally do less well.

When the Inner London Education Authority began to publish secondary-school examination results, it devised a statistical method of measuring what schools were achieving against what they might be expected to achieve, given their intake. TGAT has suggested that when schools publish assessment results at 14 (and earlier in the primary schools) they also offer parents some explanation of their circumstances so that their examination performance may be put in perspective and fairer comparisons made.

But it is not even quite as simple as that. When Professor Michael Rutter and colleagues looked at schools in similar areas with similar intakes in 1979, they discovered that there were marked differences in the effectiveness of schools which appeared to have little to do with their social composition or the attainment of their intake. In other words, as parents have always suspected, the school itself, rather than simply social or family background, was making a significant contribution to the performance of children. What needs to be measured to give an indication of the effectiveness of the school in raising the performance of its children from wherever they have started at 11 is the 'value added' by the age of 16. In other words, in terms of the National Curriculum, an inner-city school where the 11-year-olds come into secondary education having attained only level 3 in most subjects and which raises the performance of most of them to level 8 over their five years in school, may be proving itself considerably more effective than a more privileged suburban school whose pupils are generally on level 5 at the age of 11 but leave five years later at level 9. School A will have pushed its pupils up five levels of attainment, school B only four.

This sort of analysis is not easy to make. Few secondary schools yet have any consistent measure of the attainment of their intakes. Yet without that, any direct comparison of school examination or test results is a very dubious statistical exercise which may mislead parents profoundly about the effectiveness of a school. If the National Curriculum assessment system is eventually introduced as now proposed, it could have some interesting consequences. Schools and parents will then know exactly what incoming pupils have achieved and what gain is made in subsequent years. Comparisons will be possible not only between schools but internally, giving for the first time an opportunity to discover how far schools are able to raise performance overall and also whether they are diminishing the differential between those who make most progress and those who make least – the major objective of the equal opportunities policies which justified the introduction of comprehensive schools, and which are currently claimed to underlie the National Curriculum and other initiatives like TVEI. The aim is said to be a levelling-up of standards for ethnic minorities, girls and working-class students, all of whom currently lag behind in some respects. It remains to be demonstrated.

Academic attainment is in any case only one of the objectives of secondary education. When parents, students and employers in Kent were asked by the local authority to list the four attributes of secondary schools they rated most highly, parents and children came up with good teaching, good discipline, good exam results and preparation for good citizenship. Employers were not surprisingly more utilitarian in their expectations and put job preparation top, with good exam results not figuring at all amongst their top four concerns. Such expectations indicate how the 'consumers' are likely to try to judge school quality, and only in the case of exam results will they generally have anything other than subjective evidence upon which to base their judgements.

Education research has come up with other indicators for schools which are likely to prove effective – although none is an obviously easy aspect of a school for an outsider, like a visiting parent, to weigh up during a short visit. The Inspectorate has always emphasised the crucial role of the head in a 'good school'. Professor Peter Mortimore suggests twelve key factors, not listed in any order of priority: purposeful leadership by the head, the involvement of the deputy head or heads, the involvement of the rest of the staff, consistency amongst teachers, structured lessons, intellectually challenging teaching, a work-centred environment, a limited focus or set of objectives in each teaching session, maximum communication between teachers and parents, good record-keeping, parental involvement in the school and a positive climate, in other words an atmosphere which encourages success and achievement and does not demotivate the slower learner.

Parents are not the only people anxious to measure the quality of school life. The Department of Education and Science has taken two separate approaches to the problem. The first has been to make a pilot study of methods of appraising the performance of teachers in six local authority areas. This entails reviewing the performance of all teachers, including heads, with regular classroom observation, and the provision of in-service training for staff found to have problems. The Inspectorate reported that appraisal schemes they had surveyed had had a marked effect for the better on the performance of individual teachers, and on the management of schools. The report on the pilot scheme, which recommended implementation by 1994, was greeted with approval by the teaching unions but further progress on a full-scale appraisal system, which would have cost up to £40 million and involved an extra 1,800 teachers, was postponed in the autumn of 1989 by John MacGregor on the grounds that he should give some respite to schools already heavily burdened by the introduction of the National Curriculum.

The argument that schools are overburdened by change is irrefutable, but it is also arguable that raising the quality of teaching in schools through an appraisal scheme could have done more to raise standards than any amount of curriculum change, while also providing parents with what they apparently want more than anything else – good and effective teaching. Mr MacGregor, in the face of a growing teacher shortage, declined to take that road.

But of course the further one moves away from the relatively objective but very limited outcome of examination results, the harder it is to evaluate how a school is performing. The DES's second approach to the problem was to try to develop a set of 'performance indicators' quite apart from academic results by which schools could be judged. At various stages it was suggested that these might include truancy rates, the proportion of pupils in trouble with the police, the pupils' 'demeanour' coming in and out of school, the proportions of school-leavers unemployed and staying in full-time education, and much more. Unsurprisingly, this sort of proposed 'measurement', much of it as dependent on the social and family circumstances of a school's pupils as on the school itself, raised much resentment amongst teachers and heads. At the time of writing, the development of DES performance indicators seems to have quietly run into statistical sand. On questions of discipline and social development parents will, it appears, be left to make their own judgements for a little longer.

So just what are the prospects for better secondary schools in the 1990s when standards are so hard to evaluate and the attempts to raise them so many and varied? Even the most optimistic supporter of government policy in the late 1980s would probably admit that the prognosis is mixed. The Department of Education and Science invented the term 'innovation overload' for the situation schools found themselves in after the passing of the 1988 Act, and it is a situation which will continue as the major features of the Act – curriculum change, new assessment procedures, greater competition between schools and new forms of management within them – come into force. All these aspects of the Act are intended to raise standards, but all, as the decade begins, are still under some question politically and are being implemented in many schools amidst great anxiety on the part of governors, headteachers and staff.

At secondary level, the ultimate practicability of the National Curriculum rests simply on the availability of sufficient specialist teachers to enable schools to offer more classes in science, technology and modern languages, which are at present dropped by many students at 14. Recruitment to teacher education courses picked up in the autumn of 1989, but the increase in recruitment was mainly confined to courses of primary training. There was still a shortfall of recruits in maths and physics and in secondary subjects over-all. The government has responded to the shortage of second-ary staff by launching two schemes to encourage recruits without conventional qualifications into the schools, a move bitterly opposed by the teachers' unions on the grounds that this will lower rather than raise standards. The government is also attempting to attract more inactive teachers, many of them married women who have 'retired' with families, back into the profession, but this approach is hampered by the reluctance of the government to subsidise child-care schemes which could make the lot of working mothers easier.

Difficulties within the teaching profession, which lead to many talented teachers leaving in mid-career, are as much concerned with morale as with pay, although there is no doubt that a cash limit for the pay settlement of 1990 below the rate of inflation is not going to help recruitment or reten-tion of good teachers. For much of the period of the Thatcher government, ministers consistently attacked the profession for its alleged shortcomings. Teacher reaction to the legislat-ive proposals of 1988, not all of them uniformly hostile, were dismissed as special pleading and ignored in Parliament. It is small wonder that a survey in 1989 revealed the startling statistic that as many as a third of teachers would prefer to be in other jobs if they could find them. Unfortunately the teachers who can find other jobs are those with the very qualifications – in maths, science, computing and languages – which the secondary schools need most desperately and upon which the success of the National Curriculum's aim of broadening the education of all young people up to the age of 16 depends.

Nor is it yet clear whether the National Curriculum and other 1988 reforms will be funded sufficiently generously to bring about the sort of rapid rise in standards that is desired. The government backed away from compulsory appraisal of teachers not merely because it would add to schools' workload at a time of rapid innovation, but at least in part because it would cost £40 million and a lot of teacher time. Aspects of the National Curriculum will be equally expensive in terms of teacher time. And schools, facing up to the management of their own budgets in many areas for the first time, are already beginning to calculate the cost of extra specialist facilities and resources – from science labs to computers – which they will need as the National Curriculum requirements are phased in. The size of the final bill for the 1988 Act – which went through Parliament on the premise that it could be funded largely out of existing resources – is imponderable, but it is likely to be considerably larger than the DES has yet admitted or than the Treasury is prepared to fund.

As the National Curriculum working parties report and regulations are made by ministers, there are also increasing doubts about the feasibility of the entire academic structure at secondary level. There is little dissent from the initial programmes of study in the core subjects of maths and science. Nor, to judge by primary-school experience, will there be much of a problem with English. Beyond that, the difficulties of trying to pack seven or eight further subjects into the 14-to-16 timetable, and the desirability of spelling out in great detail what pupils should be taught at that age in subjects such as history and geography or art and music, will become more evident. Technology alone, which is intended to subsume aspects of design technology, business studies, information technology, home economics and design, is already causing major headaches in many schools as working parties attempt to come to grips with what is required.

Schools may balk even more as it becomes clear that the new structure will interfere with, and perhaps destroy, other initiatives which have already begun to prove their worth. It is not only teacher appraisal that ministers have apparently put on ice in order to expedite the National Curriculum. Records of achievement are not being given the priority by government which many schools wished them to have: they will take second place to the new – and as yet non-existent – assessment system. GCSE will also have to be adapted, and it is not at all clear how TVEI or the successful initiative for slow learners, the Low Attaining Pupils Project (LAPP), highly commended by HMI, will fit into the new structure. There is an alarming impression that initiatives begun in the early 1980s and now beginning to bear fruit will be sacrificed wholesale to Kenneth Baker's new and untried order, an impression which fills many good and dedicated teachers with foreboding.

The implications for standards of this level of conflict at the very heart of secondary-school practice are not hard to predict. GCSE was launched and other initiatives like TVEI and LAPP and records of achievement set up in very difficult circumstances but with a very high level of teacher enthusiasm and commitment. In many ways they were curriculum and assessment reforms which grew out of developments at school level. The National Curriculum is a top-down reform, for which little such enthusiasm is apparent in the nation's staffrooms. Whether such root-and-branch change can be effected — and effective — without commitment at the grassroots must be, at the very least, doubtful.

And at the same time as what is taught in secondary schools is put through the mincer, in the case of the 14- to 16-year-old age-group for the second time in four years, secondary schools are being asked to take on the heavy responsibility of running their own budgets, and the extra stress of competing with each other for pupils in what, in some areas with many surplus places, will become a very cutthroat market indeed.

The consensus is that given a formula for funding which takes into account the differing historical needs of schools — the nature of their intake, the state of their buildings, and their historic teaching costs — the ability of heads and governors to manage their day-to-day financial affairs for themselves will lead to greater efficiency. However it is already clear that the local management of schools (LMS) scheme being imposed by the government, and opposed by some local education authorities, will allow none of those three variables to be adequately catered for. The amount of the budget which does not have to be allocated simply according to the numbers and ages of pupils in a school is not sufficient to allow account to be taken of the numbers of special needs children or children from poorer homes a school may have and also make some allowance for the particularly small size of a school. Local authorities effectively have to subsidise one or the other, not both. Financial constraints are also making it impossible for some local authorities to bring all their school buildings up to a similar state of repair before LMS is introduced. As a result some schools will face a much greater maintenance burden than others. Others will be thrown into difficulties by the government's insistence that teachers' salaries must be funded at an average figure, not at the actual cost per school. This threatens to penalise schools with older and more stable staffs so severely that half a dozen local authorities, at the time of writing, were putting up schemes for DES approval which effectively ignored this provision in the regulations.

It is inherent in the LMS reform that some schools will win and some will lose. The rationale is that the losers will be the less effective schools which will be so galvanised by their financial misfortune that they will raise their standards, attract more pupils and balance the books. CTCs and grant-maintained schools are supposed to have the same stimulating effect. It is a market solution intended to tackle the problems of surplus school places and school quality simultaneously. But it is a market solution so riddled with financial anomalies as to make its working at best unpredictable and at worst unjust.

There is the hotly disputed question of the funding formula described earlier. There are geographical and social considerations which affect parents in urban areas just as much as in rural counties where school choice may depend on available transport. There are the difficulties of assessing school quality except by the crudest measures. And there is a system of funding schools differentially, firstly between the private schools with their assisted places and the state sector – private secondary-school fees are almost always higher than state school unit costs – and then between the burgeoning variations on the state school theme, with CTCs, grant-maintained schools and small schools all potentially if not actually funded more generously than the common-or-garden comprehensive of average size. It is small wonder that many school heads regard certain born-again entrepreneurs who have jumped on to the grant-maintained bandwagon since the passing of the 1988 Act with a mixture of incredulity and outright hostility.

What inter-school competition might achieve, though, is what the government's opponents argue is on the hidden agenda anyway: the re-establishment of a more differentiated school system, with some schools reintroducing selection, either overtly by attainment or covertly by social means. If that is in reality what the government intends, then much of the 1988 Act makes sense. But there will undoubtedly be resistance to that scenario from local authorities, heads and parents. As one head told me bitterly, he did not come into education to cut his colleagues' throats. Nor is there any evidence that in the long run, throat-cutting will in any way raise the standards of those schools which find themselves at the bottom of the competitive heap – starved of prestige, pupils and therefore funds. The reverse seems more likely.

There remains one last question to ask about the future of secondary education in the 1990s. There has emerged over the last ten years an unusual consensus between government, industry and many educationists that standards can be raised by turning the secondary-school curriculum in a more practical and 'relevant' direction. It was the philosophy which underlay much of the development of GCSE and TVEI and projects such as 'Education for Capability'. It is there, in a slightly more ambivalent form to appease the traditionalists on the government's right, in the programmes of study and assessment proposals for the National Curriculum. It runs through the development of 'profiling' and records of achievement which attempt to capture pupils' whole experience at school, rather than simply quantify their academic successes and failures. Employers have welcomed these developments and there is no doubt that as a reaction to a secondary curriculum which was over-theoretical and literary, this whole movement has had a beneficial effect on teaching methods and student motivation. GCSE has proved that clearly enough.

It seems churlish to complain about success at a time when so much of the future is shrouded in uncertainty. It seems even odder to be accusing a Conservative government of an attempt at social engineering. And yet when one considers the totality of what is proposed for young people over the next decade, with its levels of achievement, standard assessment tasks, profiling of skills and attitudes, social and personal education and economic awareness-raising, the image of a production line inevitably springs to mind. And the standardised products coming off the end of it are all too easily seen in purely economic terms as cogs in the great machine that is the UK Ltd.

Perhaps it is time to remind ourselves that secondary education is not simply about producing square pegs to fit square holes to please employers. It is about enabling young people to develop their own interests and capacities as well as fitting them for 'the world of work', to use the common phrase. It is about allowing them to try things and occasionally fail, it is about developing confidence as well as competence, creativity as well as skills, non-conformity on occasion as well as compliance. None of this is easy to define or measure, some of it is uncomfortable for parents and teachers alike, and yet without some attempt to provide it, there is a real danger that secondary schools in the 1990s will gain the National Curriculum and much else, and lose their soul. What price standards then?

INDEX